MAKING YOUR VOICE HEARD

HOW TO OWN
YOUR SPACE,
ACCESS YOUR
INNER POWER
AND BECOME
INFLUENTIAL

MAKING YOUR VOICE HEARD

CONNSON CHOU LOCKE

ENDEAVOUR

To my husband Jay

First published in Great Britain in 2021 by Endeavour,
an imprint of Octopus Publishing Group Ltd, Carmelite House,
50 Victoria Embankment, London EC4Y 0DZ
www.octopusbooks.co.uk

An Hachette UK Company
www.hachette.co.uk

ISBN 978-1-91306-820-2

A CIP catalogue record for this book is available from the British Library.

Printed and bound in the UK.

1 3 5 7 9 10 8 6 4 2

This FSC® label means that materials used for the product
have been responsibly sourced

Contents

INTRODUCTION
Why Does Upward Influence Matter?

Laura left the meeting feeling demotivated. She had wanted to add her own views to the animated discussion, but the others kept interrupting each other and she couldn't find a good time to jump in. She tried to interrupt, but her attempts were ignored. In the end, she gave up and told herself that her views were not that important anyway.

Rahul had been working at his company for 10 years and was feeling frustrated. He had seen the same problems arise year after year, and he had thought about how to fix them. He had emailed his boss with some of these ideas but did not receive a reply. The next time they met, his boss did not say anything about the email. Rahul did not want to push his luck by bringing it up, as he thought he might have overstepped his authority. Instead, he felt increasingly frustrated and dissatisfied with his job.

We can all identify with Laura and Rahul's desire to be heard, to feel as if we have influence in our work and home lives. This deep-seated human need has always existed, yet many of us still struggle to make our voices heard, especially in the hierarchical organizations and societies in which we live. When I lecture on 'Developing your presence, power, and influence' as part of the *Guardian* newspaper's Masterclass series, the sessions always sell out, which demonstrates to me the thirst for this topic. Afterwards, participants ask me for advice on specific challenges they are facing, circumstances in which they are trying to influence a person or a situation and are unable to do so. Sometimes they are not sure if they should speak up at all. Yet to thrive and succeed, organizations need their people to speak up.

Irving Janis, a well-known psychologist and decision-making researcher, coined the term 'groupthink' to refer to a phenomenon where a group makes the wrong decision because no dissenting view is expressed. Janis found this was because members either prioritize group cohesion above all else or because the group is homogenous and sees the world in similar ways. Groupthink still occurs but, with the increasing diversity of the workforce and society, a more likely reason is that dissenting views are simply not heard. Diversity in communication styles means that cultural differences and gender bias can get in the way of effective communication.

There have been many books written on influence, but they often do not consider how culture, gender and non-verbal behaviour determine whose voice is heard and whose isn't. The workshops I teach for United Nations staff cover this dynamic. I teach a workshop for mid- and senior-level female managers from various UN agencies who work in high-stress environments, for example, providing humanitarian aid in war-torn countries, helping developing countries combat poverty and educating villagers on the prevention of AIDS. The wide range of contexts in which they work means that a one-size-fits-all approach to influence is not helpful for them. In my sessions, they learn about cultural contexts and gender biases that can affect their attempts at leadership and influence, and we discuss strategies for adapting to those contexts. The participants find it eye-opening and it was at one of those workshops that it was first suggested I write a book on what I was teaching.

This book is aimed at people whose voices are not being heard or who are uncertain about how to speak up. The world is becoming more complex and difficult to navigate. We cannot continue with old ways and expect them to work in a new and changing world. Now more than ever we need to hear these diverse voices and dissenting views. Drawing on research from social psychology, cognitive psychology and sociology, this book will explain how we communicate, why we are prone to miscommunication and how to overcome these barriers in order to make an impact.

What is 'upward influence' and why does it matter?

I teach at the London School of Economics and Political Science (LSE) but before that I used to work as the Regional Training and Development Manager for the Asia Pacific offices of the Boston Consulting Group, a strategy consulting company. There, I was asked to teach the consultants how to influence their bosses. The senior executives, who were mostly Western expatriates, wanted the consultants, who were mostly locally hired, to 'push back' when discussing solutions for their clients. The senior executives knew that, without dissenting voices from the consultants who had collected and analysed the data, it would not be possible to discover the best solutions for each local environment. In these sessions, I found that some consultants appreciated learning how to speak up to their bosses. Others, however, balked at the idea, convinced that disagreeing with their bosses would be a 'career-limiting move'.

This dilemma – helping the consultants speak up to their bosses – became my focus when I went on to do a PhD in Organizational Behaviour (that is, psychology applied to organizations). I called it 'upward influence' since I was referring to employees trying to influence *up* the hierarchy rather than downwards. Upward influence can refer to any situation in which you have less power than the person you are trying to influence, for example, students influencing their teachers, members of a club influencing the president or children influencing their parents.

Growing up with strict Chinese parents, I did not have a voice. My mother once took me shoe shopping when I was in high school and rejected every option that I chose, instead choosing a pair of shoes that I was embarrassed to wear. In her defence, I never told her how I felt about the shoes (although I am not sure it would have made much difference). Coming home from my first year at university, I decided it was time to find my voice. I asked my sister, who was three years younger, to help me organize a family meeting where we explained to our parents that we wanted to make our own decisions. The meeting did not go well. They said they would be failing in their duty as parents if they let us make our own decisions since we were likely to make mistakes as a result. Nothing we said could convince them and we finally gave up in frustration. Many years later, I realized the mistake I had made: I had failed to consider the cultural difference between my Chinese immigrant parents and my American-born self (see Chapter 6 for more on culture).

As I grew up, I found myself struggling to find my voice in many other situations: at work, with friends, and even with my husband in the early years of our relationship. One night, we had agreed to sit down and discuss the plans for our wedding. But when I was ready to do so, I noticed he was in the middle of watching a movie on TV. I waited for the movie to finish but by then it was late and he said he was too tired. When I expressed my frustration he replied, 'Why didn't you tell me you were waiting for me? I would have turned off the movie – I've seen it before.' Only when he said that did I realize how much I had stifled my own voice.

When I recognized that other people also struggled with making themselves heard, I was eager to learn more about it. But I couldn't find much research on what I called 'upward influence'. There was plenty of research on influence, but nothing that specifically looked at *how* to influence people who have more power than you do. Instead, I discovered related topics such as employee voice (understanding when and why employees raise issues with management),[1] issue selling (middle managers promoting issues of personal and strategic importance to upper management),[2] and whistleblowing (employees' attempts to halt illegal or immoral practices),[3] none of which were exactly what I wanted to study. They looked at *why* people might speak up, but did not focus on *how* to do so successfully (with the exception of issue selling which I discuss in Chapter 7). I did, however, find research confirming the benefits of upward influence.

Organizations benefit from employees bringing their ideas and concerns to management, since the employees are closer to their customers and daily operations. Conversely, organizations suffer if they stifle the voices of their employees. Dissatisfied employees who feel unable to express their concerns to management wind up becoming disengaged or quitting, leaving management wondering what happened.[4] At the extreme, if employees hesitate to challenge their managers, the consequences can be life-threatening: over 80 per cent of aeroplane accidents investigated were found to involve the failure of the First Officer to speak up and correct the Captain's mistake.[5]

The benefits of encouraging upward influence can be applied outside of work too. A family that is willing to listen to the voices of the children will be a more cohesive unit and less likely to have the children act up, as I have found now that my own daughters are teenagers. It can be fun as well: one of our best family holidays was one where we let the children (who were aged ten and twelve at the time) come up with ideas for family outings.

If you are the one daring to speak up, the results can be positive for you too. Rather than the career-limiting move that the consultants feared it would be, there is evidence that it can be a career-promoting move. The consultants that I worked with in the Greater China region learned this when a European project leader (let's call him 'Max'), seconded to the Shanghai office, demonstrated the benefits of upward influence. Max was working with his team when the senior partner dropped by to share a list of demands from the client. Instead of agreeing to the demands as most project leaders would have done, Max shook his head and told the partner they needed to assess the team's workload and tell the client they could not do everything the client demanded. Talking back to senior partners (especially when they were communicating client demands) was unheard of in the region and Max's team members braced themselves for an angry response from the partner. Instead, the partner welcomed the challenge and appreciated Max's concern for his team. Max soon earned a reputation as one of the more successful managers in the region as he was able to deliver for the client without burning out his team.

A number of studies have found that if you engage in upward influence more often:

- you are more likely to receive better performance appraisals, experience greater job satisfaction and feel more committed;[6]
- you may be seen as more promotable, a better performer and more likeable;[7]
- it will not necessarily harm your reputation, even if your attempt is unsuccessful.[8]

As risky as it may seem, it appears there is more to gain than lose from engaging in upward influence. However, the outcome can differ depending on the influence strategy. People who use aggressive or manipulative tactics (for example, threats or excessive flattery) do not always reap the benefits and can sometimes encounter resistance and poorer performance appraisals.[9] In other words, simply speaking up is not enough – you must know how to do it effectively. And that is what you will learn from this book.

Upward influence – at work or at home – can be rewarding for you and those around you. Speaking up and making your voice heard can make your life more satisfying and improve your relationships, replacing silent resentment with open communication.

What will you learn from this book?

Part 1: The face you show the world

Your ability to influence others depends on the impression you make on them, especially if you are meeting them for the first time. Chapter 1 explores how non-verbal communication plays a critical role in making ourselves heard and understood. This chapter introduces the four channels of communication (kinesthetic, visual, paralinguistic and linguistic), three of which are non-verbal. It also includes tips on how to deal with interruptions, which could help Laura (whose story I told at the beginning of the introduction) make her voice heard. Chapter 2 explains how to own your space by using non-verbal communication to be more influential. In addition to learning the components of a 'confident demeanour', you will also be introduced to influence strategies such as rational and soft tactics and Cialdini's principles of persuasion.

Part 2: The inner self

If all you do is change your surface behaviour, then the changes will be superficial and short-lived. To make real changes in your ability to be influential, it is important to consider your inner self. Chapter 3 helps you develop your inner power through understanding your power bases and building your reputation, resilience and self-confidence. You will also learn strategies for managing your emotions to ensure they help rather than hinder your influence attempts. Rahul will find helpful advice in this chapter for overcoming his hesitancy to approach the boss. Chapter 4 draws attention to the voice inside our heads, that internal voice that can either help us or undermine our efforts to be more influential. You will discover the undermining thoughts that are most common, and how to overcome them and replace them with an inner voice that strengthens and guides you instead.

Part 3: The social context

There is no such thing as a one-size-fits-all approach to becoming more influential. Our ability to influence others depends on how our behaviour is perceived and those perceptions vary with context. Behaviours that we have grown up with and assume are universal – standing patiently in a queue, not interrupting someone who is speaking – are norms that vary greatly according to culture and gender. If we fail to understand this, we hamper our ability to influence people from diverse backgrounds. Chapter 5 examines gender and influence. You will learn about the 'leader prototype' that results in men often being seen as more influential than women and will find out why gender stereotypes are just as harmful for men as for women. Chapter 6 explores cultural differences that are most relevant to upward influence: power distance (the degree to which people accept and expect that power is distributed unequally) and communication style. This chapter will explain how these cultural differences might affect what you do and how to adapt to different cultural contexts.

Part 4: Creating positive change

What if we are doing everything right but we still seem to be bumping up against an invisible wall of resistance? Chapter 7 looks at the psychological barriers that might affect the person you are trying to influence and how you can deal with them. The second half of the chapter provides an easy reference tool that organizes the advice from the entire book and brings it into one place.

Start your journey

In the well-known Aesop's Fable, the North Wind and the Sun were arguing about who was more powerful and decided to have a contest to settle the question once and for all. They saw a lone traveller on the path below and agreed that whoever could make the traveller take off his coat would be the more powerful one. The North Wind went first, blowing as hard as possible and making the trees shake. The man hunched over and pulled his coat more tightly around himself. Then the Sun took over, shining softly and spreading warmth over the land. The man relaxed and, after a while, started sweating and took off his coat. The Sun had won.

This fable is used to illustrate the effectiveness of soft tactics such as persuasion (the Sun) over hard tactics such as brute force (the North Wind). But I also find it to be a good illustration of the difference between power and influence. Both the Wind and the Sun had power, but only one of them had influence because only one of them used the right strategy. If you want to be more influential, you must work on both your *internal power* and your *external influence strategy*. This book helps you do both.

Becoming more influential is a journey that requires motivation, self-awareness, persistence and practice. This book is intended as a companion to help you on that journey. Come back to it often, re-read the parts that are relevant to your specific challenges and eventually you will notice improvement. Enjoy the journey.

PART 1

THE FACE YOU SHOW THE WORLD

CHAPTER 1

Communication Is More Than Words

Marie volunteered to be a school governor because she wanted to influence the running of her children's school. But when she walked into the first meeting, she felt uncomfortably small. The attendees were mostly men and the only other woman in the room was much taller than she was. She shrank in her seat and stayed silent for most of the meeting. Whenever she tried to make a point, no one noticed her tentative attempts and she left the meeting wondering if she had made a mistake in signing up.

Kai had been working for an American company for several years and his English had improved a great deal since he started. Yet he was frustrated that he could not speak as quickly and smoothly as his American colleagues. He struggled to find the right words and often hesitated and stumbled. His boss told him to be more confident, but he did not know how.

Influence is a combination of the message and the way in which we deliver that message. If we cannot deliver our message so that other people notice and hear it, then we will not be influential. The *non-verbal* aspects of communication – the elements that are not the words themselves – are just as important as the actual message.

We instinctively know that the way we deliver a message is important – why else would we invest in presentation skills training and purchase books on body language? But if we focus only on body language then we are limiting our understanding of communication. There are actually *four* channels of communication – *linguistic* (words), *paralinguistic* (voice), *kinesthetic* (touch and proximity) and *visual* (appearance) – and body language is only one of them. Just as powerful is the voice. Listen to a professional storyteller and you will notice that they use much more than gestures to illustrate the story. Watch a powerful speaker such as Martin Luther King Jr and you will notice he hardly uses his body at all as he stands behind the lectern. Professional storytellers and powerful speakers hold our attention through their voice: the cadence, pauses, intonation, volume and other vocal qualities. Of course the words are important as well, but we must not forget how the voice, face and body can change the impact of those words.

If Marie and Kai adopt the confident non-verbal signals we discuss in this and the next chapter, Marie is more likely to be noticed and Kai will appear more confident. Kai can also benefit from some of the tips for non-native English speakers in English-speaking companies later in this chapter (and both of them need to work on building their inner power as discussed in Chapter 3). You'll see throughout the book I use the term 'native speaker' to refer to a person who speaks the dominant language of a particular country as their mother tongue. While this term is considered contentious by some, it is the shorthand commonly used in research on this topic.

Out of the four channels of communication, three are non-verbal. By understanding all of them, you can increase your impact and ensure that your message is heard.

Is non-verbal communication really that important?

You will find countless websites which claim that '93 per cent of communication is non-verbal!' While this has a grain of truth, it is not completely accurate, as is often the case with much psychological research that finds its way into popular culture. This claim originates from research by psychologist Albert Mehrabian who was trying to determine the relative impact of different channels of communication.

Mehrabian and his colleagues compared three of the four channels of communication: words (linguistic), vocal tone (paralinguistic), and facial expression (visual). They were using pre-recorded presentations so didn't study the impact of touch and proximity (kinesthetic). In the study, actors varied their facial expression and tone to indicate a positive, neutral or negative attitude, while keeping the words the same; participants were asked to judge the speaker's true attitude. In such a scenario, you can imagine the words did not contribute much to perceptions of the speaker's true attitude. If someone says to you, 'I like your haircut' and you are trying to figure out their true attitude, how much would you pay attention to their words? Hardly at all! You would be listening to the tone of their voice (paralinguistic) and looking at their facial expression (visual).

This is exactly what Mehrabian found: that words count for very little when someone is expressing an attitude.[1] He estimated the following equation for the impact of the communication: *7 per cent words + 38 per cent vocal qualities + 55 per cent facial expression.*[2] This led to the popular belief that communication is 93 per cent non-verbal – but remember that this is only true when communicating an attitude, feeling or opinion. If you are giving a factual account, then your words will count far more than 7 per cent. But if you are expressing an attitude such as, 'your presentation was good' or 'I am excited about this project', then be careful. Simply saying the words will not convince anyone because they are looking for the non-verbal cues. If there is a mismatch between the words and the non-verbal cues, the listener will believe the non-verbal cues, not your words.

TIP: If you are communicating an attitude or opinion, be especially careful that your non-verbal signals match your words. If you are unsure, ask a friend or trusted colleague to watch you communicate that attitude or opinion and then ask them if you came across as sincere. Any inconsistency and it is your words that will be held in doubt. Because non-verbal signals are more difficult to control, people often assume they are a more accurate reflection of your true feelings than your words.

Even when we are not expressing a feeling or attitude, non-verbal signals can have an impact on the impression that listeners form of a speaker. Imagine listening to the CEO of your company deliver the most important speech of the year – what aspects of the speech will affect your opinion of the CEO? One group of researchers decided to explore this when they recorded a fictitious CEO giving a speech and varied the content of that speech (visionary versus non-visionary), delivery (strong versus weak non-verbal cues) and success of the organization (high versus low performance). Out of those three factors – content, delivery and performance – delivery turned out to have the biggest impact on how charismatic and effective the CEO was judged to be. In other words, it did not matter how well the organization performed or what words the CEO used; if the CEO delivered his speech in a strong and confident manner, people judged him to be more effective and charismatic.[3]

Non-verbal signals can also have an impact on the way others react to your message. When my children were toddlers, we had the usual parent–child struggle at bedtime. When I said, 'get ready for bed', they would both refuse – but the way in which they each said 'no' triggered very different reactions in me. One said it in a defiant, angry way while stamping her foot. The other one said it calmly, with one hand to her chin, as if I had made a suggestion that was unworthy of her consideration. This disarmed me and even made me laugh, lightening the mood. Their words were the same, but the way in which the children delivered that word changed its impact. Such is the power of non-verbal communication.

How do I improve my communication skills?

Let's start by exploring the four channels in more detail.

• Words matter, but not as much as we might think

Getting the words right is important when we are sending a letter or email – that is, when we are exclusively using the linguistic channel of communication. But when we are speaking, the exact words we use become less important because meaning is also conveyed through our non-verbal signals. While we seem to understand this in conversations, focusing on our meaning rather than exact words, we often forget it when we engage in public speaking.

Most people find public speaking highly stressful and they try to control that stress by focusing on the words they will say. I have seen presenters spend hours working on language rather than the message or delivery, even choosing to read from a piece of paper to ensure the words are exactly right. Reading from a piece of paper is acceptable if you are speaking for only a few minutes – for example, when introducing the main speaker – but doing so for half an hour makes the talk less than engaging. The words might be exactly right, but does that matter if people have stopped listening?

> **TIP:** Instead of creating a script for yourself, think about the key messages you want to deliver and the desired outcome of your communication. What are your key messages? What do you want the audience to think or do differently? If you have these two things clear in your mind, then the words will flow.

'I've learned that people will forget what you said, people will forget what you did, but people will never forget how you made them feel.' This oft-repeated quote from Carl W Buehner, erroneously attributed to Maya Angelou,[4] reminds us that words are often forgotten. Think about the last time you heard someone give a presentation. Do you remember the exact words that were used? Probably not. We tend to remember the meaning and feeling conveyed by the presentation rather than the actual words. This should hopefully be comforting to nervous presenters and non-native English speakers working in English-speaking companies. I have taught presentation skills to many non-native English speakers, some of whom are so self-conscious that they end up speaking in a halting manner, correcting themselves and feeling that they are not speaking properly if their grammar is slightly wrong or their words are not perfectly chosen. But humans are not particularly good at remembering words; we tend to remember images, stories and feelings.

Nonetheless, we cannot ignore the immense power of words. A disorganized or confusing narrative will be poorly received, no matter how strong the delivery. To make yourself more engaging and charismatic, use the linguistic techniques identified by social psychologist John Antonakis and his colleagues.[5] These include employing metaphors, stories and anecdotes. The positive feedback that I get from people who attend my lectures or talks often mentions the anecdotes I use to illustrate my points. Audiences find the anecdotes engaging, memorable and helpful in driving home my key messages. These anecdotes usually come from my personal experience, which includes living in different countries and working in a wide range of companies.

Aside from personal experience, you can also glean anecdotes from the experiences of other people; for example, reading interesting biographies, listening to interviews or even socializing widely with a diverse network.

Antonakis also found that leaders appear more charismatic if they express moral conviction, use contrasts and rhetorical questions, and communicate high expectations of their followers as well as confidence that they can meet those expectations. These devices tap into the audience's emotions, making the presentation more powerful. In order to be perceived as charismatic, however, these linguistic techniques need to be combined with non-verbal cues such as an animated voice, gestures and facial expressions.

TIP: Use metaphors, stories and anecdotes to illustrate your key points. Storytelling is a highly engaging way of communicating (provided the story is relevant and concise!), and stories leave listeners with images and feelings they will remember long after your words have faded. Prepare for a presentation by thinking of relevant stories, anecdotes and metaphors rather than by wordsmithing.

Of course, if you are sending an email or some other form of written communication, it is worth spending extra time choosing the precise words and phrases. Emails are an efficient tool for co-ordination with co-workers and straightforward messages. However, emails use only one out of four channels of communication, so it is hardly surprising that they are often misunderstood. Words spoken with a different tone can mean very different things – and it is difficult to convey tone in an email. The 'tone' that you hear in your head while writing the email will not necessarily be heard by the person reading it. Sarcasm or humour do not transmit well in an email. If you are sending a message that is likely to elicit negative emotions in the recipient (critical feedback, for example), it might be better to pick up the phone. A phone conversation offers you two channels of communication (words and voice) which will convey your tone and give you the chance to hear their reaction and adjust your message accordingly. A video call could be even better, allowing you to supplement your message with facial expressions. If you need a written record, send a follow-up email summarizing the conversation.

It may be especially tempting to use email when you are angry as it gives a false sense of being rational and objective. I can think of several occasions when I was upset with someone and wanted to send them an email detailing what they had done wrong and how they needed to fix it. But using only one channel of communication when giving negative feedback can inflame the situation and result in multiple emails of escalating anger and defensiveness (something I learned the hard way!). Nowadays, I pick up the phone or arrange a meeting. Speaking in person allows us to engage in a dialogue, resolve the issue more quickly and preserve the relationship. It allows me to find out their perspective on the situation before I jump in with accusations and assumptions. I have learned that listening to the other person first can often change my perspective on the situation and lead to a better outcome – but this type of dialogue is not possible over email.

> **TIP:** Don't use email indiscriminately. Think about the purpose of your communication and consider if it might be better to pick up the phone or arrange a video call.

• The power of the voice is often neglected

It is not often that we take time to think about the paralinguistic aspect of communication, yet it covers a surprising amount of territory. It includes any sounds we make that are not actual words, such as laughing, sighing, saying 'uh' or even the lack of sounds, such as hesitations and pauses, that occur while we are speaking. And it includes the characteristics of our speaking voice, such as volume, tone, pace, accent and pitch. For example, we can speak quietly or loudly, timidly or confidently, in a halting or fluid manner, in a monotone or with varying pitch and emphasis.

Varying our pitch and emphasis is something we naturally do in conversation but it often disappears when we engage in public speaking. Many people become more monotonous when they are presenting and then return to a more natural and expressive speaking style during the question-and-answer session at the end. When I coach people in presentation skills, I film them and show them the contrast between their presentation voice (monotonous) and the voice they use to answer questions (expressive). The goal is to deliver the presentation with their more natural-sounding and expressive voice. One tip I gave a particularly monotonous presenter was to read storybooks to his young children in order to learn how to be more expressive – I thought the exercise would help him learn to modulate his voice a bit more.

Modulating your voice not only makes it more engaging, but it can also help convey your message as you emphasize key elements and de-emphasize others. It could even make you sound more intelligent as a more expressive voice is associated with greater intelligence.[6] But avoid overdoing it. I once heard a speaker whose voice was so expressive that it made her sound as if she were speaking to children (the audience were all adults). It sounded like a parent trying to hold their toddler's attention by overemphasizing every word ('And AFTER the FIRST STUDY, we ran ANOTHER ONE and found the SAME RESULT!'). How can you figure out the right level of expressiveness? Experiment and get feedback.

TRY THIS: Using modulation to sound more engaging

Practise with a three-minute excerpt from a presentation (or passage from a book) and record each attempt. Push yourself to the extremes of expressiveness, both low and high. First, speak as monotonously as possible, then speak in an overly dramatic manner (exaggerate and have fun with it!), and finally, speak with a degree of expressiveness somewhere in the middle. With the dramatic extreme, go crazy and really push yourself. This exercise should feel uncomfortable – you are aiming to sound more engaging, not stay within your comfort zone.

Trying out these extremes will help you sense where the middle lies. This does not necessarily mean that the middle is your ideal. Try a few different points between the two extremes. If you are a very monotonous speaker, you might even find that your extremely dramatic voice sounds surprisingly normal and is the right level of expressiveness. Play the recordings for your friends or colleagues and get feedback from them.

Another highly noticeable quality of the voice is the accent, especially a foreign accent. These days, the language of business is primarily English, regardless of where you live in the world. Even if the company you work for does not come from an English-speaking country, they might choose English as the language of business, as the French employees of a French multinational discovered to their dismay.[7] Being forced to communicate in English can feel like a disadvantage to non-native English speakers who may feel discriminated against because they do not speak English fluently or because they speak with a foreign accent.

Research on prejudice and discrimination has tended to find that people with foreign accents are perceived more negatively by native speakers, and the stronger the accent the more negative the evaluation.[8] This bias against people who speak the local language with a foreign accent is true not only in English-speaking countries, but also in other countries (Sweden, Germany and Guatemala are a few of the countries where this was tested). But this doesn't always lead to discrimination – unless the listener already has an underlying prejudice against foreigners.

Remember, however, that your accent is only one small part of how you communicate. The studies cited above only found that *on average* people with accents were perceived more negatively – this does not mean that everyone was perceived negatively. There are many other aspects of communication that you can use to manage others' perceptions of you, including appearance, vocal expressivity and the content of what you say. Harvard Business School professor Laura Huang and her colleagues tried to understand the reason behind the negative perception of foreign accents and they found it was because some native speakers assumed the foreigner was not familiar with local culture and therefore less able to navigate subtle and complex social interactions.[9] Huang found that foreign-accented entrepreneurs in a pitch competition who gave examples of navigating complex social situations (such as closing a deal or negotiating preferential pricing) were often more successful than native English speakers.[10]

TIP: If you speak with a foreign accent and are being interviewed for a job by native English speakers, it might help to provide examples of your ability to navigate complex social situations or examples of how your multicultural background gives you an advantage in the role. For example, if you are applying for a teaching job, you could point out that your own experience as an international student has taught you how to create a more inclusive classroom environment, and that you are able to make concepts easy for all students to understand.

An example of someone who speaks with a foreign accent yet exudes more confidence than many native speakers is Jia Jiang, a Chinese man in the US who created the website *100 Days of Rejection Therapy.*¹¹ The website contains short videos of Jia Jiang making unexpected requests of strangers in order to desensitize himself to the pain of rejection.

> **TIP:** Do not be overly self-conscious of your accent as this can affect your confidence. Instead, remember that most people are more interested in what you have to say rather than the accent with which you say it. If your accent is affecting comprehensibility, then make an effort to speak more clearly, but otherwise focus on your message and non-verbal demeanour. Learning to adopt a confident demeanour, which we will discuss in the next chapter, can make you appear more charismatic, competent and effective.

'Filler words' are words or sounds that do not add meaning (*um, uh, like, y'know*) and are used as a kind of verbal tic, unnecessarily filling in any silences. We might think that filler words indicate to others that we are still speaking and therefore prevent them from jumping in, but they are more distracting than helpful. I once listened to a speaker who used such a long and drawn-out 'uuum' that I stopped paying attention to his message and instead found myself waiting for the next 'uuum'. If you worry about being interrupted, it is better to say gently, 'let me think…' or 'give me a moment…' Filler words are best replaced with a brief silent pause because they tend to occur frequently and only for a split second. Pausing between thoughts is good practice anyway, as it allows your listener to take in what you have just said. Deliberate pauses in a presentation can even make you appear more confident – but only if you accompany the silences with a 'confident demeanour' (see Chapter 2). Otherwise, you might appear to be hesitating rather than intentionally pausing.

TRY THIS: Using pauses to sound confident

Return to the three-minute excerpt that you worked with earlier (see page 15). This time we are going to explore the power of pauses. Start by recording the excerpt at your natural pace. Then do it again, pausing intentionally at key points (after an important piece of information; after completing a thought), holding each pause for around two seconds. If you use filler words, replace them with a brief silence instead. If you have been told that you speak too fast, do not slow down your speech as that can feel – and sound – unnatural, but speak at your natural pace and insert pauses. The pauses allow your listeners to catch up mentally with what you are saying. Get feedback from your listeners to see if it helps, and adjust the number and length of pauses accordingly. Listen to the difference this makes in your delivery.

The tone with which you deliver a message is a particularly important aspect of the voice to learn to control because it can change the meaning of your words. The same sentence ('great job on that project') can sound congratulatory or sarcastic depending on how it is delivered. Learning to consciously manage the tone of your voice will help you become a more influential speaker by making the meaning of your message more clear and impactful.

TRY THIS: Conveying meaning through tone

With a friend, take turns saying the sentences below in the two different ways, without revealing your intended meaning. In addition to vocal tone, use facial expression to help convey the meaning:

Sentence 1: 'Great job on that project!'; first in a congratulatory tone, then a sarcastic tone.

Sentence 2: 'What do you think of this idea?' in an uncertain tone (as if you think it is a bad idea) and then in a confident tone (as if you think it is a good idea).

Your friend has to guess which meaning you are trying to convey. Go back and forth, taking turns and giving each other feedback to hone your vocal tones and facial expressions. The key to sounding sincere is to avoid overdoing it when you are, for example, trying to sound congratulatory. These sentences are just suggestions – feel free to create your own examples as well. The goal is to manage your voice and face to the point where your meaning becomes crystal clear.

The voice is an incredibly powerful tool that can make us more engaging and confident-sounding. Yet most of us do not use it to its full potential. Take time to revisit the exercises in this section on a regular basis. Keep the recordings that you make so you can review your progress. Of the four channels of communication, this is probably the one that has the most untapped potential for most people. Spend time mastering paralinguistic communication and you will differentiate yourself from other speakers.

• Touch and proximity require sensitivity to the other person's comfort level

If you are working remotely and communicating through emails and video calls, spend time honing your paralinguistic skills – your voice is the main channel through which to engage others when you cannot tap them on the shoulder or look them straight in the eyes (see the Resources section on page 251 for tips regarding video calls). But when you are in the same location as others, then your use of the physical space around you can be a powerful way to communicate. Standing closer to someone and turning towards them can indicate concern, while stepping back and turning the body away can convey a desire to disengage. A gentle touch on the arm expresses sympathy, while a firm pat on the back provides encouragement. When we meet a stranger, we often draw conclusions about them based on the firmness of their handshake – and that first impression tends to linger.

How many of us ask for feedback on the quality of our handshake or enquire whether we are standing or sitting too close to someone? For most of us, myself included, it seems awkward to ask and easier to assume the other person's level of comfort is the same as our own. Yet each person's level of comfort can vary widely. Where one person might greet with a hug, another might prefer a handshake. Even the same person's comfort level can vary, sitting closer to a friend while leaving more distance with a colleague.

Proxemics is the study of how we use the space around us, especially the amount of space we feel necessary to maintain when interacting with another person. As you might expect, there are cultural differences. When I worked in Hong Kong, I often attended cocktail parties with guests from all over the world and it was not uncommon to experience an inadvertent 'dance', with one person moving closer and the other person stepping back as a result of differences of comfort with interpersonal distance. Anthropologist Edward T Hall was one of the first to notice these differences and his research found that cultures where people tend to stand closer include South American, Southern and Eastern European and those in the Arabic-speaking world, while the cultures where people tend to stand further apart include Asian, Northern European and North American ones (of course, these are broad generalizations that are not true of every country or individual).[12] He believed there was a particularly stark difference between Arabic and North American cultures, noting that Arabic people felt the distance at which North Americans stood was cold and aloof, while North Americans saw the distance at which Arabic people stood as intrusive and rude.[13]

TRY THIS: Gauging your own comfort level

Gather a small group of friends or colleagues. Ask one person to sit in a chair in the middle of the room (without a table or any other furniture around them). Move all the other chairs away. Now take an empty chair and pretend that you are going to have a conversation with the seated person, placing your chair at what you consider a comfortable speaking distance (do not place a table or any other object between you). Have a short conversation to check that it really is what you consider a comfortable speaking distance. If not, then adjust the chair.

Now have someone take a picture from a fixed point in the room where they can easily see the distance between the two chairs. Move your chair away and have the next person do the same thing. Again take a picture.

By the end, you should have a series of pictures showing where each person decided to place their chair. See how much variation there is in the group. If you are all the same gender and from the same cultural background, there might not be much variation. But in a more diverse group you should notice some differences. Ask the stationary person which distance they preferred and if there were any that made them feel uncomfortable.

If there was variation, notice whether you tended to sit closer or further than the others. This will tell you something about your own comfort level and give you some guidance on how to approach strangers. If you have a tendency to sit closer than others, perhaps hold back a bit in case the other person feels uncomfortable. If you have a tendency to sit further than others, make yourself move in ever so slightly to avoid appearing too standoffish. Test this out on your friends to see how they react.

Hall also noticed differences in the propensity to touch others while interacting. 'High-contact' or 'expressive' cultures not only stand closer when speaking, but they are also more prone to use touch during conversations. One of my Greek students, for example, has a habit of touching my arm to punctuate what she is saying to me. In contrast, Northern European, North American and Asian cultures tend to fall towards the 'low-contact' or 'reserved' end of the scale (again, these are generalizations as there are country differences and even regional differences within the same country). While expressive cultures often greet with a hug or kiss, reserved cultures greet with a handshake. Some reserved cultures avoid physical contact altogether, especially between men and women, by replacing the handshake with a bow or nod. In India and Thailand, the standard greeting is a head nod accompanied by a praying hand gesture called a 'namaskar' or 'wai'.[14] When travelling, be aware of the local practice so that you can adjust accordingly (most travel books provide this information).

> **TIP:** Before travelling to another country, find out the local practice for greeting others and use it. Most people appreciate this as it shows you have taken time to learn about their culture and respect their customs. However, be aware of individual differences. If the person is young and educated overseas, they might think the local custom is old-fashioned and prefer a simple handshake. Follow their lead.

Using touch and proximity for influence means making the other person feel comfortable with you. This requires a keen sensitivity to their comfort level and expectations. Sit too close and you might be perceived as being too intimate; too far and you might be perceived as being cold. Whenever possible, try to let the other person take the lead and adjust accordingly. While in many cases it is safer to be more reserved, especially with the opposite sex, in an expressive culture being too reserved might make you appear less approachable. The kinesthetic channel can be a difficult one to use well, especially cross-culturally, but if you can master it, it will help you create stronger connections with others.

• Appearance is most important when making a first impression

As you might imagine, your appearance can convey a great deal of information. When we meet someone, we very quickly form a first impression, which includes taking in their physical characteristics, clothing, posture, stance and facial expression.

The visual channel is a powerful one, so powerful it can affect our other senses. Imagine listening to an instructor's voice with an unidentifiable foreign accent. Would the instructor's appearance make a difference to how you perceive the voice? In a study of university students in the US, the answer was yes. Students who were shown the picture of a Chinese instructor rather than a white instructor rated the same voice as having a stronger accent.[15] The visual channel also affects the way we taste and experience things. When the same cheap wine was bottled in two different ways – as a California wine and as a North Dakota wine – customers at a restaurant had very different experiences. People who were given the bottle with the California label enjoyed the wine, drank more of it and lingered at their meal. People given the North Dakota version said the same wine tasted bad, drank less of it and even found the food less tasty.[16]

Just as the label on a bottle of wine can affect our judgement of its taste, a job candidate's appearance can affect our judgement of their suitability for the job. Researchers found that job candidates tend to receive better evaluations if they use eye contact, smile often and lean forward. But other aspects of appearance had an even bigger impact on interviewers' impressions: the candidates' business attire, grooming and physical attractiveness.[17]

> **TIP:** When preparing for a job interview, role-play
> with a friend to practise making eye contact, smiling
> and leaning forward. Record yourself to see the
> impression you make. On the day of the interview,
> make sure your hair is neat and you are wearing
> appropriate business attire. Remember that there is no
> 'standard' business attire that applies to all industries.
> If you want to be seen as a good fit with the company,
> find out how they dress. One of my students once
> showed up for an interview at an advertising firm in a
> conservative grey suit, only to discover the employees
> were wearing more colourful outfits. She didn't get
> the job.

The fact that physically attractive job candidates can make better impressions is related to a concept called the 'beauty premium', a term coined by economists David Hamermesh and Jeff Biddle. In their 1994 study, Hamermesh and Biddle examined data from large household surveys conducted in the US and Canada that included a rating of attractiveness by the interviewers who collected the data. They found that more attractive people tended to earn higher hourly wages. While attractiveness is largely subjective, studies such as these find that multiple independent judges will generally agree on the attractiveness of a particular person based on elements such as facial proportions and balance.

More recent research has found that when personality and grooming are also considered, the beauty premium disappears for women and weakens significantly for men.[18] It also seems that people use attractiveness as a substitute for ability only when actual ability is not known. In a lab experiment, participants were shown photographs of candidates and asked how much they would offer them for a job involving bargaining or data entry. The beauty premium only occurred when the person was being hired for a task in which attractiveness was relevant (bargaining, but not data entry). After the person's actual job performance became evident, the beauty premium disappeared.[19] Attractiveness was used only when better information was not available.

Rather than focusing on the beauty premium, we should focus on job performance, grooming and other elements of our appearance such as body language, clothing and facial expression.

Remember, too, that in many cases appearance matters most only when making a first impression. Over time, your personality, integrity and capability will become apparent. Appearance is most important when we do not have better information – once we know more, appearance becomes less important.

Even when making a first impression, appearance is not everything. I learned this lesson the hard way as a novice corporate trainer. I spent the night before my first big training session agonizing over my outfit and perfecting my Powerpoint slides when I should have been clarifying the purpose and key messages of the session. Even though my outfit and slides looked great, the session turned out to be mediocre, with poor structure and unclear messages. I have since learned that balance is critical: appearance may be important but influence also requires confidence and a clear message. In fact, as we will see in the next chapter, appearing confident can convince others that you are also competent and effective. Perhaps more important than the beauty premium is the 'confidence premium'.

How do I make the most of conversations?

When we are in conversation with someone else, we often assume they are using the same unwritten rules regarding when to interrupt or whether to ask questions. However, professor of linguistics Deborah Tannen observed differences in conversations at work, especially between women and men.[20] Women tend to use a more self-deprecating and group-oriented style, deflecting compliments, saying 'sorry', asking questions and saying 'we' instead of 'I'. In contrast, men tend to use a more self-promoting and individualistic style, announcing their accomplishments, avoiding apologies, making statements and saying 'I' instead of 'we'. These differences are not surprising. Girls and boys learn different ways of interacting with the world through the games they play and the expectations of the people around them. Girls are expected to be more co-operative and boys more competitive.[21] In other words, our societies contain separate female and male sub-cultures, each with their own unwritten rules about communication. These unwritten rules are taken on by teams, organizations and other groups. Groups that are male-dominated often adopt a more competitive style of communication; female-dominated groups adopt a more co-operative style.

If you are not aware of the unwritten rules, it becomes more difficult to be heard. As Tannen observed, women tend to wait their turn to speak while men tend to interrupt each other. Of course this is not true of all women and all men; there will be a great deal of variation. But it is helpful to know that some people interrupt more than others, ask questions more than others or brag more than others. Realizing these are socially learned behaviours rather than personality traits can help you to be more flexible with your own behaviour. If you find yourself in an environment where people are constantly interrupting each other and you insist on waiting your turn, you will never be heard. If you are accustomed to asking many questions and continue to do so in a meeting where you are expected to sound confident and certain, some people may assume you are not knowledgeable enough to be in the room.

> **TIP:** When you find yourself in a new context,
> pay attention to how the people around you are
> communicating. Adjust your communication style in
> the same way you would adapt to a different culture.
> The more you can adapt, especially in meetings
> and group conversations, the better your chances
> of having your voice heard. If you don't like the
> culture and want to change it (for example, to stop
> people from interrupting), you first need to establish
> credibility with your colleagues by building your
> power bases (see Chapter 3), then you can start
> to influence change.

• Learn to handle interruptions

A female executive once complained to me that she found it difficult to contribute to meetings because her (mostly male) colleagues kept interrupting. But when I suggested that she learn to interrupt as well, she was offended by my advice. Her socially learned views of interrupting were so deeply ingrained that she simply could not find it acceptable. Yet there is a great deal of variation among cultures when it comes to interrupting. While more reserved cultures find interruptions rude, expressive cultures consider frequent interruptions a normal part of conversation. A study of a Swedish–Spanish negotiation found that, compared to the Swedes, the Spanish interrupted five times more often.[22] At the other extreme, the Japanese not only avoid interrupting, they will even wait several seconds before speaking to ensure the other person is finished. Expressive cultures can interpret this as the speaker not having anything more to say and jump into the silence. Interruptions are a culturally learned behaviour and the more we can understand and accept this variation, the easier it may be to adjust our own behaviour to fit the context.

What if you are the one being interrupted – how should you react? Essentially, you have three options:

(1) Stop talking and cede the floor, or

(2) Pause and acknowledge the interruption then continue, or

(3) Ignore the interruption and keep talking.

A fourth option, if you are in a context where interruptions are the norm, is to cede the floor (Option 1) but only temporarily, jumping back in to make your point. Your choice of option will depend on the context and type of interruption.

TIP: To choose the best response to an interruption, consider the context. If you are in a brainstorming meeting and someone more senior interrupts your half-formed idea with their own idea, it might be best to cede the floor (Option 1). If a colleague interrupts asking for clarification, respond to the interruption, clarify and continue speaking (Option 2). Option 3 is the one to use with chronic interrupters who do not allow you to finish. You can either keep talking and ignore them or turn to them and say 'just a moment' in a firm but friendly manner before continuing. Or say something light-hearted such as, 'I'm glad you're so excited by what I said, but I haven't finished yet.' The key is to avoid getting angry. Staying firm but friendly will get you further.

It can also help to identify an ally (or allies) in the group – people who agree to stand up for each other so that, if one is interrupted, the others will step up and say, 'hold on, I'd like to hear the rest of what (s)he has to say.' If the chronic interruptions are caused by one specific person, you could take that person aside for a private chat, explaining how their interruptions make you feel and asking them to please wait until you have finished your point. The chronic interrupter might have grown up in a context where interruptions were the norm and have no idea how their behaviour is affecting you. Of course, this will depend on whether your relationship with that person is good enough for you to give them candid feedback. The point is that interruptions are a learned behaviour which means we can learn to adjust if necessary.

> **TIP:** Finding allies to help stand up to chronic interruptions is especially helpful for women in a male-dominated environment. Not only are women more likely to be interrupted in such an environment, but their ideas are sometimes ignored until a man repeats the same ones. In that case, allies can say, 'that's great that you're picking up on Lisa's idea. I think it's a good one, too.'

• Stop apologizing when you don't need to

The word 'sorry' deserves a special mention here. Deborah Tannen found that women tend to say 'sorry' more often than men in situations where it is not necessary; when you could say 'excuse me', for example, or when it is actually the other person's fault (though I have found many men in the UK also say 'sorry'). 'Sorry' is a powerful word as it shows deference to others and can reduce your status. Using it too often can make you appear weak and timid, as if you are apologizing for existing. One of my daughters developed this habit and her sister helped her break it by asking, 'why are you saying "sorry"?' whenever she said it unnecessarily.

Please do not misunderstand me: I am not suggesting that we never say 'sorry'. But it is a powerful word that should be used consciously, not in a habitual, unthinking way. If I am late to a meeting and I am one of the more junior people in the room, then I will say 'sorry I'm late' as a way of showing deference to the others. On the other hand, if I am the most senior person and am chairing the meeting, I will say, 'thank you so much for your patience!' 'Sorry' should be reserved for the times when it is really needed. Apologizing for yourself all the time can create the impression that your voice does not deserve to be heard.

> **TIP:** If you have a habit of saying 'sorry' too often, replace it with a more appropriate word. Search the internet for 'what to say instead of sorry' and you will find plenty of good suggestions such as in a Catalyst article.[23] It suggests thinking about the intention behind 'sorry' and using those words instead. If you want to show empathy say, 'how frustrating for you...' (instead of 'sorry you were stuck in traffic'). If you want to interrupt, say 'excuse me'. The best advice I have seen is to replace 'sorry' with 'thank you', as in 'thank you for waiting.' It shows appreciation for the other person and maintains your status.

Whether or not you interrupt others, the way you handle interruptions and your tendency to use 'sorry' can affect the way others perceive you. Being more aware of the way you use these conversational techniques will help you become more influential.

Do we pay too much attention to non-verbal cues?

Unlike words, non-verbal cues can never be switched off; even when we are sitting still or not thinking about anything, someone observing our behaviour can still (mis)interpret our posture or facial expression. How often have you jumped to conclusions based on the way someone is sitting or the look they have on their face? I remember a man who attended one of my talks and looked like he was scowling the whole time. As I was speaking, I wondered what I was saying that was making him angry. After the presentation, he raised his hand and I braced myself for what I thought would be an antagonistic comment. To my surprise (and relief!), he told me how much he had enjoyed the presentation and then asked a question for clarification. I had completely misinterpreted the expression on his face, which was probably just his natural resting face!

My misinterpretation is not surprising. Even though we often try to guess what others are thinking and feeling, we tend to overestimate our ability to read others' minds. Nonetheless, we continue to give it our best shot. In doing so, we often rely on non-verbal cues because not only are they always active, but we often think they reveal the person's true feelings. Even after living together for more than twenty years, I can still misunderstand my husband's facial expressions, thinking he is upset about something when he is not. Rather than misinterpreting those signals, I have learned to suspend judgement and tell myself, 'don't jump to conclusions!'

How can we apply the advice in this chapter to Marie and Kai? For Kai, the emphasis should be on developing the other qualities of his voice such as modulation, pauses and tone, and to use more anecdotes, stories and metaphors. By focusing his listeners on stories and images, he will draw their attention to the content of his message. Marie, on the other hand, needs to make herself seem bigger and more confident. While the advice in this chapter is a good starting point, her main focus should be on the next step: owning her space and demonstrating a confident demeanour.

Let's take what you have learned so far about non-verbal communication and bring it to the next level. In the next chapter, you will learn how to put these non-verbal signals together in a way that will make you appear more confident, competent and powerful, and you will learn how to combine this with influence strategies to make you more persuasive.

CHAPTER 2
How to Own Your Space

Before going to the next school governors' meeting, Marie gathered a group of friends for a role play in which she learned how to get the group's attention and make her point. Her friends gave her feedback and she practised until she felt more comfortable. With the role play fresh in her mind, Marie felt determined when she arrived at the meeting and sat down. She adopted the confident demeanour she had recently learned, sitting up straight with her hands planted wide. She forced herself to look around the room, making eye contact and smiling at the other members, and even chatted with those sitting nearby instead of staring at her phone. Making these pre-meeting connections helped her get noticed once the meeting started and one of her neighbours even jumped to her rescue when she was interrupted during discussions.

As Marie demonstrated, owning your space is a combination of appearing confident through non-verbal signals and being able to connect with the people around you. This chapter covers both. But why does confidence matter so much? And what exactly are these non-verbal signals that we should be using? Let's find out.

Why does confidence matter so much?

After living in Hong Kong for ten years, I moved to California to obtain a PhD and was called up for jury duty. As a non-white female student who looked younger than my age, I should have had a relatively small degree of influence in the group. My view was in the minority, shared with only one other person on the jury. However, the non-verbal cues (eye contact, posture, confident tone of voice) I had honed during my years as a corporate trainer – combined with the logical argumentation I had learned as a management consultant (also called 'rational influence tactics', discussed later in this chapter) – helped convince the group to see things my way.

Why would being a non-white, young-looking female student normally mean that I have less influence on the jury? Because those characteristics are not associated with status. Sociologists have studied the ways in which we grant influence in a working group and found that characteristics deemed to be associated with status, such as education, occupation, gender, ethnicity and age, are found to have influence in a group.[1] Imagine participating in an experiment where you are serving on a mock jury and must decide the amount of money a plaintiff will be awarded. Nobody in the group has expertise that is directly relevant to the case. During the discussion different views arise, and the correct answer is not clear. How would you decide who to listen to?

In most cases, the person with the most influence on the group decision is the person who has more education, works in a more prestigious job or belongs to a dominant group such as being male or white. This is not conscious or even logical behaviour on the part of the group: if a medical doctor is on the 'jury', that person will have more influence on the final decision than other group members, even if the issue has nothing to do with medicine. Of course, a person may have more than one status characteristic. In a group comprised of a white male construction worker, a black male investment banker, a white female computer technician and a black female teacher, who would have the greatest impact on the group's decision? Most likely the black male banker as he has the combined status of being male and in a high-paying prestigious job.

The idea is that you and the other jury members are trying to ensure a successful outcome and, because you do not know each other's actual competence, you use these visible characteristics as a proxy for competence. If someone has qualifications specific to the issue at hand, that characteristic would be used instead. For example, if the decision concerned computers, the female computer technician would have more influence (though not as much as a male technician). The longer a team has worked together, the more likely they will be to focus on specific characteristics such as knowledge and skills rather than surface characteristics such as gender and ethnicity.[2]

The good news is that even if you don't possess what are considered high-status characteristics, you can still have influence. My own experience on a real jury is an example of this. The key is to look and sound confident because confidence is a status characteristic that anyone can use.[3] Confidence is used as a substitute for competence when actual competence is not known – hence the reason why being too forceful does not work. Dominating someone by staring or using a loud and commanding voice does not signal confidence and therefore does not give you more influence. In a group where you are not the boss, appearing confident is far more effective than appearing dominant.[4]

An added bonus to looking confident is you will also be perceived as being more powerful and leader-like because the non-verbal cues associated with confidence are the same as those associated with having power. Imagine visiting an office and seeing two co-workers standing in the corridor speaking to each other. One is standing with legs planted solidly apart and arms gesturing outwards, while the other person hugs a pile of paper tightly, their body contracting. The first person speaks louder than the second person and interrupts a few times, while the second person speaks with some hesitation. Who do you think is the more senior person? Most people would immediately say the first person. This is because the non-verbal cues associated with power are widely recognized. People with power (the boss or teacher, for example) tend to have a more open and expansive posture, lean in to the other person, interrupt more often and speak louder compared to people with less power (the employee or student).[5] These cues also signal confidence – in other words, by looking confident, you also make yourself look more powerful.

How can I look and sound more confident?

During the role play, Marie had struggled. Daunted by the prospect of trying to get the attention of strangers, she kept forgetting what her friends had taught her about looking confident. But her friends would not give up. 'Look around the room,' reminded one of them. 'You sound too tentative; speak more confidently,' reminded another friend. 'Sit up straight and unfold your arms,' reminded a third. By the end of the afternoon, these behaviours were coming more naturally. She watched a video of herself from the beginning of the afternoon compared to one from the end and could see how much she had improved. Watching herself look so confident even gave her an internal boost of confidence and she felt ready for the next school governors' meeting.

The behaviours that Marie was learning are the same behaviours I used to teach in presentation skills training. But are these behaviours actually supported by research? Yes they are, I discovered when I went on to do a PhD – but only very few of them. Mastering the surprisingly short list of non-verbal signals – what I call a 'confident demeanour' – is enough to make you appear more confident, powerful and influential. These behaviours are grouped below into three categories: eye contact, vocal qualities, and posture and gesture.[6]

• Eye contact while speaking should be at least as frequent as eye contact while listening

If you were to watch a video of two people having a conversation but with the sound turned off, would you be able to tell which person has more power in the relationship? Social psychologist John Dovidio and his colleagues found the answer to this question is often 'yes' because people instinctively observe the 'visual dominance ratio'. This ratio measures the difference between *looking while speaking* and *looking while listening*. The person with more power (the boss or teacher) tended to make eye contact while *speaking* more frequently than while *listening*. The opposite was true of people who had less power in the relationship (the employee or student), who tended to make eye contact while *listening* more than while *speaking*. When peers were speaking to each other, the ratio was almost equal.[7]

We often think of eye contact as a one-dimensional behaviour, but Dovidio's research tells us otherwise. Eye contact while *listening* is good because it conveys warmth and attention. But eye contact while *speaking* is critical for power and influence.

> **TIP:** Use frequent and regular eye contact, especially while speaking. This does not mean non-stop eye contact – it is natural for our eyes to wander as we think. But if you find yourself avoiding the other person's gaze while you are speaking, then catch yourself. One of my students said she struggled with eye contact because it felt too intense to stare at the other person's eyes. In fact, 'eye contact' does not mean staring directly at their eyes – it means gazing at the eye-region of their face with 'soft' eyes (a less direct gaze that allows some peripheral vision). This should feel more natural and less intense. When speaking to an audience, I let my eyes rest on different parts of the room, turning my face so that everyone feels I am speaking in their direction.

• Your voice should be audible with a confident tone and fluid pace

In the previous chapter, you practised modulation, which is important for speaking in an engaging manner (see page 15). If you want to speak with confidence and power, then also pay attention to volume, tone and pace.

Volume refers to being easily audible; speaking too softly can give the impression of weakness. Of course, volume needs to be adjusted to suit the size of the audience and room. In a small office with three colleagues, you will need to speak more softly than in a large room with fifty people. If you find that you are constantly asked to repeat yourself, you might be speaking too softly. The best way to find out is simply to ask.

> **TIP:** Ask a trusted friend or colleague after the meeting if your volume was appropriate. If you want to practise, go back to the same meeting room with your friend and speak at different volume levels. When you hit the right volume, try to remember how it felt so you can reproduce it.

In the previous chapter, I offered an exercise for 'Conveying meaning through tone' (see page 20) that included saying a sentence in an uncertain versus confident tone. Try it again with a different partner to see if you can consistently convey your meaning to others. The exercise is challenging because you are also required to ask a question in a confident tone. A confident tone implies that you are sure of what you are saying; using it to ask a question makes it even more difficult.

TIP: With a confident tone, your sentences should end with a definite stop in your voice and a pitch that slightly drops. Notice if your voice is trailing off at the end of a sentence or rising as if you are asking a question. Both can make you sound uncertain.

A fluid pace means speaking at a natural pace with few hesitations or stumbles – but there should be regular pauses. In the previous chapter, I discussed using pauses to sound confident (see page 19). If you need more practice, revisit that exercise. One thing you might have noticed is that inserting pauses will reduce the time available for you to speak. To compensate, reduce the amount of material you will cover and present it in a more succinct manner, focusing on the key points. Less information with more emphasis on each point is a good strategy, as your audience is more likely to remember your key messages.

TRY THIS: Explaining the key points succinctly

Take one of your presentations and turn it into an 'elevator pitch'. This means that you have to explain it so succinctly that you could do it in the time it takes to ride in an elevator with the boss. To do this, organize your thoughts in a pyramid structure: the top of the pyramid is the main topic and purpose of the presentation; branching downwards are the three or four key points. These are the elements of your elevator pitch (to make sure you have identified the key points correctly, continue branching downward from each key point to cover the detailed streams of information supporting that point). Once you know the key points, think of metaphors, stories and anecdotes to make each of them more memorable.

• Your posture should be open and gestures confident

Standing with an open and expansive posture and using confident gestures will make you appear more powerful. This is because an expansive posture is a sign of power and dominance in the animal kingdom, from peacocks spreading their feathers to primates raising their arms. We are not seeking to come across as dominant; rather we are aiming for a middle ground of appearing confident and competent. To find that middle ground, it may help to visualize the two extremes. Imagine two people sitting next to each other: Person X sitting with arms and legs close to their body, feet tucked under the chair, contracting and appearing smaller than they are, and Person Y sitting with one arm spread across the back of the chair, feet planted wide, expanding and appearing bigger than they are. The images may come to life more vividly if you imagine Person X as a timid woman and Person Y as an arrogant man. In other words, these two postures are gendered – and neither one is ideal. Instead, the goal is somewhere in the middle, taking up space while avoiding the two extremes. This is the person who conveys confidence without being domineering.

> **TIP:** Expansion (and contraction) involves movement in the shoulders, head, arms and legs. In order to find the middle ground when it comes to finding an expansive posture, try out both extremes, first contracting as much as you can by tucking your arms and legs into your body, taking up as little space as possible, and then expanding your body as much as possible, spreading your arms, legs, feet and shoulders to fill as much space as you can. Once you have physically experienced both extremes, you will

find it easier to understand what the middle

ground feels like.

Confident gestures that illustrate or emphasize the message you are delivering (for example, using the space in front of you to indicate the three phases of a project) will make you appear more powerful. In contrast, gestures such as fidgeting (jiggling a pen or shuffling papers) and self-touch (rubbing your face or playing with your hair) will make you appear less powerful. These types of gestures convey anxiety or nervousness. One of my colleagues once asked for my advice because, even though she felt confident lecturing, she had been told she looked nervous. When I watched her from the back of the lecture hall, I noticed she had a habit of playing with a strand of hair while speaking. She was unaware of this habit, but the gesture did indeed make her appear nervous.

TIP: Don't think too much about which gestures to use. Just keep your hands empty and available, hanging at your side or clasped in front of you, and they will naturally start to move when you have a point to make. Many people use gestures in conversation, but suddenly become stiff when speaking to a large audience. Bringing your natural gestures into a presentation will usually make it

appear more natural and engaging. Film yourself

to see if your natural gestures are engaging or

distracting. Get feedback from a friend as well,

as we can often be overly critical of ourselves.

Does the confident demeanour apply across all cultures? Yes and no. Within most cultures, the person with more power (the boss or teacher, for example) will use more eye contact, sound more confident and stand more expansively compared to the person with less power (the employee or student). But comparing bosses across different cultures will reveal differences in the way these behaviours are exhibited, with some bosses taking up more space than others or using more eye contact. In other words, these behaviours are universal signals of power, but the ways in which they are exhibited will vary depending on the culture.

Can a person be powerful and influential without using a confident demeanour? Yes, but that person would need other qualities that attract respect and status. I once worked with a senior consultant who was socially awkward yet highly respected. Anyone who worked with him quickly understood how he had reached the highest levels of the organization despite lacking a leader-like demeanour: he had an intimidatingly brilliant mind. His reputation for being able to get to the heart of a complex problem faster than anyone else preceded him; clients and consultants were eager to work with him and saw past his awkward demeanour. For the rest of us normal human beings, however, a confident demeanour is an important part of being influential.

At this point, you might be worrying about your own non-verbal demeanour and wondering how you come across to the people around you. While it is important to find out how you come across (through feedback or videos), do not become too self-conscious. The situations in which non-verbal behaviour matters the most are those in which the audience does not know your actual competence or when you are expected to look confident and leader-like. Start by focusing on those situations to avoid putting too much pressure on yourself. Over time, the confident demeanour will feel more natural to you and it will be easier to use more often.

> **TIP:** Rather than being self-conscious all the time, focus on your non-verbal behaviour in these two situations: (1) when making a first impression, such as in a job interview or with new colleagues or (2) when giving a presentation. In the first situation, people are trying to gain insight into your abilities, which means they will look for signals of competence, and in the second situation, you are in the spotlight and subject to scrutiny.

What else should I know about the confident demeanour?

• Narcissists are great at looking confident

The narcissist's ability to appear naturally confident may be why people who have known narcissists a short time perceive them as being leadership material, but people who have known them longer do not.[8] A study of managers in retail stores found that more narcissistic managers had had less experience when hired, a testament to their ability to make a good first impression. But the true nature of the narcissistic manager was revealed over time: the more interactions that staff had with narcissistic managers, the less likely they were to perceive them as being effective.[9] In other words, looking confident might get them in the door, but actual competence is still required.

Be vigilant to avoid being fooled by a narcissist's confident demeanour and assuming they are competent when they are not. The potential for this mistake increases in interview situations because you are meeting someone for the first time and assessing them on very little information. If you are tasked with interviewing someone and they appear impressively confident, ask for concrete examples of accomplishments – and find out how they treated the person who ushered them in. If their examples of accomplishments sound dubiously heroic and if they were rude or dismissive to the junior person bringing them in, beware. Narcissists' sense of superiority and self-absorption will often come through in the narrative about their successes and their treatment of those they perceive as being beneath them. They are also overly sensitive to perceived criticism, becoming defensive and sometimes verbally aggressive (blaming and criticizing) as a result, though this might not come across in an interview.[10]

> **TIP:** When someone strikes you as impressively confident, dig deeper. Ask more questions about accomplishments, follow up with checking references and speak to people who have worked with the person.

• Too much confidence can be seen as arrogant

Power can be thought of as a scale, ranging from *timid/weak* at one end to *arrogant/dominant* at the other end. Just as being domineering is not an effective influence strategy with peers, being arrogant is also not effective. Arrogant people tend to be less liked and less respected.[11] Unfortunately people who appear arrogant might not realize it because the point at which a confident demeanour becomes arrogance is not always clear.

If we think of arrogance as occurring on the same scale as confidence, then arrogance is essentially excessive confidence. However, whether or not behaviour is 'excessive' can be entirely down to the situation. Behaviour that is 'just right' in one context might appear 'too much' in another context. For example, an investment banker working in New York City will have adopted a confident demeanour suited to that context (perhaps speaking with a tone that is so confident it precludes further discussion) – but the same demeanour might appear overconfident or arrogant in a different cultural context, such as in the UK, or in a different industry. I had been using this fictitious example in my lectures when I met an American man who had actually experienced this. After attending one of my lectures, he told me he used to be an investment banker on Wall Street and had moved to London to work for a not-for-profit organization. At his first performance review, his English supervisor told him he came across as arrogant, a criticism which surprised (and upset) him. It was only after my lecture that he understood why he had come across that way.

TIP: If you have moved from a highly competitive, aggressive environment to one that is more co-operative, you are at risk of being perceived as arrogant in your new context, especially if you were successful in your old context. Get feedback from colleagues to find out. If that is the case, tone down your confident demeanour and get more feedback. In particular, dial down the certainty with which you speak and act and adopt a more participative communication style (pausing to ask, for example, 'what is your view on this?').

• A confident demeanour is not helpful in all situations

While a confident demeanour is useful for upward influence, it might be too much for some downward influence situations (that is, communicating 'down' the hierarchy to someone with less power). This is because the power dynamics and purpose of such an interaction are different. As the boss, you will probably have no trouble being heard, so the challenge becomes encouraging the more junior person to speak up. Imagine a situation in which you and one of your team members have both been gathering data and you now need to reach a joint decision. My research found that in such situations, a confident demeanour stifles the employee's voice and leads to a poor joint decision. Because the boss appears confident, the employee assumes the boss is also competent and is less likely to question the boss's conclusions or share information that brings those conclusions into doubt.[12] Combining a confident demeanour with signals of openness helps to mitigate this problem.

TIP: If you are trying to get one of your team members to speak up, especially if you want them to challenge you, combine your confident demeanour

with openness. Non-verbal signals of openness
include nodding, making eye contact while listening,
and asking them what they think.

How do I influence others beyond using a confident demeanour?

In my experience with jury duty, my influence on the other jurors was a result of using a confident demeanour *and* logical argumentation. While non-verbal behaviours matter a great deal, influence strategy is also important. Here I will share with you some influence strategies and how to deploy them.

• Use rational and soft influence tactics

Influence tactics fall into three categories: hard, soft and rational tactics.[13] *Hard tactics* are based on pressure, such as making threats or invoking the authority of more senior managers – for example, demanding to speak to the manager of a shop because the staff did not provide adequate service. *Soft tactics* are based on the relationship with the other person, such as appealing to friendship or loyalty – asking a friend to help you out 'for old times' sake', for example. *Rational tactics* are based on logic and information, such as appealing to the other person's interests and reasoning – asking a friend to help you out because it will benefit them as well.

Research has found that rational tactics are the most effective. Not only do they tend to be the most frequently used, but they are also the most likely to lead to desirable outcomes such as being evaluated in a more positive way and receiving a higher salary.[14] At work, you are expected to be rational and logical, and even outside of work it is effective, as I found when serving on the jury. We are often at our most convincing when we use information and logic to back up our arguments. However, rational tactics by themselves can appear cold. Combining them with soft tactics in a sincere way can create the interpersonal connection needed to be more influential.[15] Imagine you have been asked to reduce the membership of a committee. Here are two different messages for the members who are being let go:

Message 1 (rational): 'We would like to inform you that the goals and needs of this committee have changed, which means the composition of the committee must change and your services are no longer needed.'

Message 2 (rational and soft): 'Thank you for serving on this committee. You have made important contributions to the direction and quality of the project and we really appreciate it. Unfortunately, the goals and needs of this committee have now changed, which means the membership of the committee must change. While you will no longer be a member of the committee, we nonetheless welcome your input going forward.'

While the first message is more efficient, its abruptness could cause the recipients to feel offended and question the decision, resulting in several follow-up messages, or they might resent you and the decision, leading to future tension. Taking time to write the longer message, which shows appreciation for the people, could save time and avoid harming the relationship with them. Of course, the effectiveness of the longer message depends on whether the recipients will actually feel appreciated, so avoid making it sound like an insincere form letter. Personalizing the message often helps, giving a specific example of something that you appreciate about them or their contribution. Delivering the message in person would be even better, as you would give them a chance to respond, but that is not always practically possible.

> **TIP:** Soft tactics, such as showing appreciation, require a thoughtful and personalized approach. Be specific about the behaviours or qualities that you appreciate in order to come across as genuine.

If you lack the information required for a more rational logic-based approach, it is possible to use soft tactics alone. This involves focusing on each person and the relationship, including exchanging favours, appealing to friendship or complimenting the other person. A sincere approach to establishing a connection can increase their willingness to co-operate. If you do not have a good relationship with the other person, however, soft tactics will not work. In a relationship characterized by conflict, attempts to use friendliness or flattery are likely to fail and may be interpreted as being manipulative. Even in a good relationship, using soft tactics carries the risk of appearing manipulative – and manipulation can trigger resistance.

> **TIP:** The success of soft tactics depends on the quality of your existing relationship and the other person's perception of your intent. Soft tactics are less likely to work if the other person does not like or trust you because they might interpret your attempt as being manipulative and insincere.

Hard tactics are not usually helpful in upward influence situations since they are characterized by aggression and intimidation, for example, issuing threats, asserting authority and employing sanctions. If you have less (or equal) power than the person you are trying to influence – your 'target' as we call it in the research on power and influence – trying to threaten or intimidate them is likely to create resistance or even retaliation. To use hard tactics in such a situation, you need to enlist the help of others, by bringing in more senior managers or gathering a group of allies, for example, to form a coalition and apply pressure (if this group does not apply any pressure but simply makes the boss aware that many people support this idea, that would be a rational, not hard tactic). To be successful, any such group has to use a combination of pressure and protection. That is, it must be large enough and strong enough not only to force the boss to comply but also to protect individual members from retaliation – workers' unions are an example of such a group. However, beware of psychological reactance, which can occur when someone feels excessive pressure.[16] Reactance is different from resistance as it involves the person not just refusing outright, but doing the opposite of what you want. Imagine you are buying something at a shop and paying at the till. As you pull out your money, you hear the person behind you mumble, 'hurry up!' Rather than do that, some people might slow down instead – a classic case of psychological reactance. Applying pressure might trigger reactance, causing your target to do the opposite of what you want them to do. In upward influence situations, using hard tactics is risky: you risk not only failing to achieve the desired result, but also possibly damaging the relationship and your reputation as well.

To recap, when trying to influence someone, start with rational tactics, gathering the data and information that you need to make a convincing logical argument. If there is no reason for the person to dislike or distrust you, adding soft tactics will help you connect with the other person and make them feel appreciated as this will create fertile ground for your request, making it more likely to be considered. If all else fails, hard tactics are the last resort but such tactics require the help of others. Be careful, as there is no turning back from a hard tactic and the relationship with the person you are trying to convince is likely to be permanently damaged by such aggressive tactics.

• Use the principles of persuasion to convince the other person

In his classic book, *Influence: The Psychology of Persuasion*, psychologist Robert Cialdini identified six psychological principles by which we can influence others.[17] These are different from influence tactics in that they tap into natural human tendencies, getting us to comply without thinking. He developed these principles by observing professional marketers and sales people, and analysing their strategies. Becoming familiar with these principles is helpful not only so that you can use them yourself, but just as importantly so that you can protect against having them used on you. Since these strategies can be powerful, it is important to use them with ethical and positive intentions (a warning that Cialdini includes in his book). The strategies themselves are merely tools that, like a hammer, can be used to build or destroy.

I've summarized here the six principles of persuasion and how to use them:

1. *Liking*: the desire to help someone we like. Develop rapport with the other person by offering a sincere compliment or mentioning something you both have in common.

2. *Reciprocity*: the obligation to repay others in kind. If you do a favour for the other person or offer them something they want, they will feel they owe you something in return.

3. *Authority*: deference to someone in a position of authority. Give yourself the semblance of authority by convincing the other person you are an expert on the issue or you are backed up by an expert.

4. *Scarcity*: the belief that something is more valuable if it is scarce. Convince the other person that they are being presented with a rare opportunity and must act now.

5. *Social proof*: the tendency to follow the crowd. Show them that others are already doing it and they might be missing out (the fear of missing out is so widespread that it is commonly referred to as 'FOMO').

6. *Consistency*: the desire to remain consistent in our words and actions. Get the other person to voluntarily state an attitude

or belief that will lead to the behaviour you desire, for example, getting them to say they care about employee well-being before telling them about your proposal for a wellness programme.

We often use these principles instinctively, tapping into the principle of Liking when we find out that we went to the same university as the boss and use that to develop a stronger rapport with them. We are subconsciously using the principle of Authority when we back up a claim by citing an expert. While these principles are fairly straightforward, Reciprocity and Consistency require a bit more explanation.

Reciprocity is presented by Cialdini as a universal human tendency, but there are individual differences that can be described by looking at the categories proposed by psychologist Adam Grant: givers, takers and matchers.[18] If you go to your friend's house for dinner and bring a bottle of wine, and then invite that same friend to your house for dinner, what you get in return may vary depending on their personality. A giver might bring you two bottles of wine, a matcher might bring you a bottle of wine of the same value as the one you took – and a taker might arrive empty-handed and hope you don't notice. In other words, if you do a favour for someone and expect them to return that favour later, make sure that person is a giver or a matcher, not a taker. While these psychological principles are generally true, they do not affect everyone in the same way. As this book will remind you over and over again, humans are amazingly diverse in personality, which makes influencing them a complex and challenging task.

The principle of Consistency was once used on me by a British Red Cross fundraiser who came to my door. I was about to turn him away when he said, 'wait, let me ask you a question.' We then had the following conversation:

Fundraiser: Did you learn First Aid when you were in school?

Me: Yes, I did.

Fundraiser: Did you find it useful?

Me: Yes, it was very useful. I still use some of it now.

Fundraiser: Do you think children should learn First Aid in school?

Me: Yes, of course they should.

Fundraiser: Then please support our drive to get First Aid taught in schools.

At that point, I was stuck. Not only had he reminded me of my appreciation for learning First Aid in school, but he had done it in such a friendly way that I also found him likeable. In order to stay consistent with my stated view (and because I liked him), I ended up making a donation.

Finally, I want to share an example of using these principles in a message that I crafted when I worked as a training manager in a consulting company. Here, I am asking my boss for a larger training budget for the following year. I have labelled each principle of persuasion that I used in the message:

'Remember how the client complained last year that our consultants did not know how to interpret company financial data and you said you were committed to making sure that problem was fixed? Well, I found a new training vendor who can fix that problem [*Consistency*]. This vendor is used by one of our biggest competitors and I have heard positive feedback about them from other consulting firms as well [*Social proof*]. If we want to use them, we need to book them in quickly as they are very popular [*Scarcity*]. But, as you might expect, with a better-quality vendor, we will need to pay more. I can cut back on expenses for social functions to help make up for this [*Reciprocity*], so that overall our annual training budget will increase by about 10 per cent next year. Let me know what you think.'

> **TIP:** When developing your influence strategy, review the six principles of persuasion to see which ones might be most relevant for that situation. Test out your strategy by role-playing with a friend and getting their feedback.

Owning your space involves exhibiting a confident demeanour and deploying the most appropriate influence strategies. These require practice and, as we saw with Marie, engaging in a role play with friends can be a helpful way of practising and getting feedback. But this is only the first step to becoming more influential. Non-verbal signals and influence strategies are tools. If you do not have the muscle to wield those tools, they are useless. The next part of this book focuses on the 'muscle' or internal power that you need in order to wield these tools of influence effectively and make a real impact.

PART 2

THE INNER SELF

CHAPTER 3

How to Access Your Inner Power

People who meet me now will encounter a self-confident, middle-aged woman who does not balk at giving a lecture to a room full of strangers. Few of them would guess that as a teenager I was so painfully shy that I hid behind a book most of the time and was constantly being pushed by my teachers to speak up in class. When I started working, I would often sit in meetings silent – not because I had nothing to say, but because I could not get up the courage to say it. A thought would strike me, but instead of jumping in, I would wait for a lull in the conversation that never came. The longer I waited, the more nervous I became about speaking up. The moment would pass and my thought would no longer be relevant to the discussion. Now, more than twenty years later, I do not hesitate to speak up in meetings, jumping in when a relevant thought strikes me. Sometimes I'm even one of the more vocal people in the room. My younger self would not recognize who I have become.

On the surface it might seem that I have simply become more confident with age, but it is not the mere fact of ageing that has granted me inner power. Rather, it is the experiences, the challenges and even the failures that have accumulated over time and created who I am today. While each person's journey is unique, there are common denominators that can help all of us develop that inner muscle to make us more influential. In this chapter, I share with you the elements that helped me develop my own inner power.

What do I mean by inner power? Part of it is the emotional and mental strength that give us the courage to speak up, such as self-confidence and resilience. Part of it is the personal reputation that gives us the platform for speaking up, also called bases of power. Both parts can be intentionally developed, but it takes time. Unlike the influence strategies from previous chapters which can be learned and deployed relatively quickly, building inner power – like building muscle – requires persistent effort over a period of time. If you have not invested the time to build those muscles, they will not be available when you need them.

I'm going to start by discussing the bases of power or platform that you can build for yourself to ensure that you are heard and then provide tips for finding the courage to use that platform.

How do I get noticed and heard?

When Mark's boss announced in the team meeting
that she was going to save money by eliminating the

department's end-of-year party, Mark feared it would be a big mistake. He had seen in his previous company how important such events were and he suspected the minor cost savings would not be worth the amount of ill-will such a move would create. But he also knew that his boss was unlikely to take him seriously – he was too new and he had made a couple of mistakes in the report that his boss had reviewed last week. His colleague Rachel had been around a long time and was well respected. Mark invited Rachel to lunch and shared his concerns about their boss's plan. Rachel agreed with Mark and said she would raise those concerns with the boss.

If your attempt at influence is aimed at a particular person, the relationship that you have with that person will play an important role in determining your success. This may seem obvious, but many people lose sight of it when caught up in the desire to make a particular point. To them, their message is so logical, obvious or important that it supersedes the perception of the messenger. But this is wishful thinking. Influence is an interpersonal process and we cannot take the 'personal' out of 'interpersonal'. Mark knew he did not yet have any power with his boss. Enlisting Rachel's help was an effective short-term solution, but Mark now needs to focus on building his bases of power, so that in future he can approach their boss himself.

In 1959, social psychologists John French and Bertram Raven proposed a model of influence consisting of five Bases of Social Power: Coercive, Reward, Legitimate, Referent and Expert Power.[1] These five bases (or sources) of power have become one of the most widely used models of power among social psychologists today. You might wonder why a model from 1959 is still considered relevant today. This is because the fundamentals of human psychology have not changed much over the years, in the same way that human physiology has not changed much. We still need food and water to fuel our bodies, though our caloric and physical needs have been modified for modern living. In the same way, the sources of power remain the same, though their application is modified by context. The model can be – and has been – applied in any context: at home, in school, in sales situations, at work. Here, I introduce the five bases of power with an emphasis on the two (Referent and Expert) that are most relevant for upward influence.

• Coercive Power: *inducing fear from threat of punishment*

If Rachel wanted to use coercive power to convince her boss not to cancel the end-of-year party, she would threaten her boss with punishment or retaliation. Punishment can include anything the other person fears, ranging from personal rejection to going on strike. If you're laughing at the absurdity of Rachel threatening her boss in this way, you can see why coercive power is not the most useful in upward influence. When the other person has more power than you do, it is unlikely that you will have access to any punishment that they truly fear. Even if you do have access to those punishments, this is a hard tactic that is likely to damage the relationship and should only be used as a last resort, and only when the situation requires such drastic tactics (trying to save the end-of-year party probably does not count).

● **Reward Power:** *gaining compliance by offering desired rewards*

For Rachel to use reward power, she must have control over something the boss wants and cannot obtain elsewhere. Rewards can include anything the other person desires such as praise, a bonus or recognition. Perhaps Rachel manages the entertainment budget and can approve her boss's request for additional funds. This is similar to Cialdini's principle of reciprocity in that Rachel would be offering something in return for her boss complying with her request. But it implies a stronger source of power than simply offering an exchange – she would have to control something that the boss really wants but cannot otherwise get. We are unlikely to have this degree of control when we have less power than the other person, so reward power is not always relevant in upward influence.

- **Legitimate Power:** *tapping into the obligation to comply with authority*

Legitimate power would require that Rachel has some sort of authority with which her boss feels obligated to comply. This does not include authority that comes with knowledge or expertise, which is expert power. Instead, it is authority that comes with a formal position, such as being the budget holder or auditor. Clearly this would be difficult to use in most cases of upward influence.

Coercive, reward and legitimate power are usually associated with being in a position of power – but upward influence means that we are *not* in a position of power relative to the person we are trying to influence. For upward influence, it makes more sense to focus on the two bases of power – referent and expert power – that are accessible to everyone, regardless of their position.

- **Referent Power:**[2] *maintaining good relationships*

In order for Rachel to have referent power, she will need to have developed a good working relationship with her boss over the years, to the point where the boss wants to maintain that good relationship. In fact, this was the reason Mark chose to enlist Rachel's help: he noticed that their boss seemed to listen to Rachel's views and trust her judgement, giving her the most critical projects and letting her run with them. Rachel has noticed this too, which is why she agreed to bring Mark's concern to the boss. She knew that if she were the one to raise the issue, the boss would listen and give it serious consideration.

> **TIP:** When planning an upward influence attempt, think about the different targets of influence you might approach and assess your referent power with each of them. How much does each person like, admire or respect you? Do you have an especially good relationship with any of them? It might make sense to try that person first.

Referent power might sound similar to Cialdini's principle of Liking, but Cialdini's principle is a short-term strategy. Referent power is a long-term strategy that implies a much stronger attraction. Someone who has referent power could be seen as a role model, perhaps even placed on a pedestal. In Rachel's case, her boss might feel that Rachel is one of the most capable people she has ever worked with or one of the most trustworthy individuals she has met. Referent power is based on personal qualities and those qualities might have a different appeal for different people. For example, I might have more referent power with a Chinese woman who sees me as a female role model than with a European man. But these relationships can change over time. If I work more closely with the European man and we find we have common interests and perspectives, my referent power with him might then increase. Aside from similarities, referent power can also be boosted by other personal qualities such as passion for the work, a co-operative style, honesty, integrity, dependability and friendliness. Since power is in the eye of the beholder, especially when it comes to personal qualities, you need to know your target before you can assess (or boost) your referent power with them – though in most contexts, it is a good bet that people will value integrity, honesty and reliability.

> **TIP:** Since referent power is a long-term strategy, take time to develop good working relationships with those around you. In addition to being reliable and trustworthy, if you are trying to build referent power with your boss, find ways to make their life easier. Anticipate your boss's needs, think through the issues you are working on and bring suggested solutions. Make him or her look good in front of others.

Over time, your referent power can become a reputation that spreads across the organization or community. If you develop a reputation as someone who is great to work with, you are more likely to be invited to join committees or to be given responsibilities that result in greater visibility and contact with those outside your immediate network. This gives you the opportunity to establish relationships with a new set of people and, if you build referent power with them, your power in the organization or community will then increase. But, like a muscle, referent power requires consistency in order to be strengthened. Engaging in manipulative behaviours such as flattering the boss while being rude to the secretary or reneging on promises when a better offer comes along, can weaken the referent power you have built up.

> **TIP:** Be careful of trying to trick people as it can come back and bite you. Fooling others into trusting you might work in the short term, but people are able to detect manipulation and it will backfire eventually. I once taught a negotiation course where two participants who were business partners bragged about their 'good cop, bad cop' strategy of pressuring others into giving in. One of them would yell and make extreme demands then storm out of the room, leaving the other to apologize and encourage the shocked person into compromising. They were pleased with their strategy, but when my co-teacher and I searched for their names on the internet, we found multiple discussion boards warning people about them and their strategy. If you

want to build true referent power, treat people with respect and integrity.

To be clear, referent power does not involve saying 'yes' to all requests or invitations. Focus on those activities that are important to the organization and will move your career forward.

Women are often inundated with more requests than men because it is assumed they will be more willing to help. But this increases the risk of those women wasting time on unimportant projects that nobody else wants to do, which ultimately harms career progression.

TIP: If you receive a lot of requests for your time, ask yourself if taking on that new task will move your career forward. Being a helpful person will not necessarily benefit you because you could be spending your time on low-value activities that nobody else wants to do. If you are not sure about a task, talk it over with a friend or mentor. Even better, have a candid discussion with your boss about where you want to be in five years' time and ask for advice on how to get there. Based on that discussion, you should have a clearer view of the types of tasks to take on and the ones to politely decline.

Learning how to say 'no' in a polite and respectful way is an important skill and can even boost your referent power. Part of my reputation as someone with whom people want to work is due to the fact that I respond quickly and politely, even if it's to turn down a request. One of my colleagues once told me that someone had asked her if I might be available for an event and she replied, 'Why don't you email Connson directly? She will tell you right away if she is not interested or available.' If I were known as someone who delayed replying, responded in an unclear way or said 'yes' and then failed to follow through, the invitations would soon dry up.

> **TIP:** When saying 'no' to a request, try to offer an alternative – perhaps you have a colleague who can help them or a website or article that can answer their question. Rather than explaining why you cannot do it (which often sounds like an empty excuse), focus on helping them solve their problem. Sometimes I will give them an alternative that is less demanding on my time, such as offering to give them advice on their workshop design rather than running the workshop myself. But sometimes, when I have no alternative to offer, I simply apologize and say that I am unavailable.

• **Expert Power:** *exhibiting knowledge and expertise*

While referent power requires time to develop a relationship with the other person, expert power requires time to develop an expertise that is respected by the other person. If Rachel were to use expert power to convince her boss not to cancel the end-of-year party, it would require her to have expertise valued by the boss. Perhaps she is an expert manager who has increased the motivation and performance of her team. Or she is a financial whizz who has saved money for the company. Even if her expertise is not directly relevant to the issue, the fact that she is admired and respected for her knowledge and skills makes her opinion worth listening to.

Expert power is based on your qualifications, experience and competence. For example, you could be respected for having worked in multiple industries or different parts of the organization. Earning an advanced degree or one from a top university can also garner respect, but don't worry if you don't have this type of pedigree. Over time, it is actual accomplishments and performance that feed into expert power. During my first few years at LSE, I gained a reputation as an expert teacher, based on student evaluations and teaching awards. That led to me being noticed and invited to serve on a Strategic Plan Working Group. I was by far the most junior academic in the working group, yet my opinion was valued and heard. My expert power came not only from being a good teacher, but also from being a versatile teacher and administrator. I was able to teach undergraduates, postgraduates and executives as well as successfully run degree programmes for the different groups. This versatility was rare and valuable for the institution.

> **TIP:** Build your expert power by developing skills that are relevant to your career but also rare and valuable. Focus on becoming the best you can be at your job, building on your strengths rather than following your passion. Often, the more skilful you become, the more you will enjoy what you are doing. In fact, some researchers have found that competence and mastery can lead to passion, not the other way around.[3]

Developing that level of performance will get you noticed, and the 'halo' effect of expert power will get you heard. That is, people will listen to your views on a range of topics, not just the topic for which you are known. But reaching that level of performance requires hard work and takes time. As computer science professor Cal Newport advises in his book *So Good They Can't Ignore You*, rather than setting goals based on efficiency, notice whether what you are doing is easy or hard. Strain is good because it means you are pushing yourself. Without strain, you are not developing. This is not to be confused with the stress of overwork, which is not helpful. Strain is a challenge to your brain and ability, that feeling you get when learning a new language or skill. The strain cannot be sustained for too long and must be mixed in with easier tasks, but it will move you to the next level of mastery. Physicist Richard Feynman was considered a genius in his field but this did not come from being born a genius (in fact, his IQ was average). Instead, he challenged himself to understand important research papers and mathematical concepts from the bottom up, spending hours breaking them down until he could reconstruct them himself.[4]

> **TIP:** If you want to develop expert power, engage in tasks that challenge your ability. Push yourself to the edge of your comfort zone and then step out of it. When I was first invited to teach a *Guardian* Masterclass, the idea terrified me. These were members of the general public, not LSE students, and I had no idea if they would be open to what I had to say. But I knew it would help me develop my skills as a teacher and, the more often I do it, the less nervous I become.

Of course, excellent performance will only give you expert power if others are aware of your performance and accomplishments. If they are not, you might end up like Mary, who had been exhausting herself with multiple extra responsibilities in order to support the organization, only to find out she had been passed over for a promotion. When she approached the CEO, angry that her extra work had not been recognized, he looked at her in surprise and said, 'I never knew you were doing all of those things.'[5]

> **TIP:** In order to reap the benefits of your extra effort and accomplishments, make sure they are known to the people you want to influence. One tactic is to have a 'brag buddy': someone with whom you have a mutual agreement to make each other's accomplishments known to your bosses and colleagues. By bragging about someone else's accomplishments, you look like a good colleague and help that person to avoid looking arrogant or boastful. You can do this casually when chatting with others ('Hey, did you hear that...?') or by sending that person a congratulatory email while copying in their supervisor. In my position as Programme Director, I send a thank-you email to the teachers who have done a particularly good job on my programme, copying in the Head of Department.

Referent power works hand in hand with expert power because your reputation as a good colleague can generate invitations to join different committees and projects. If you perform well, your reputation as someone who is not only good to work with but also knowledgeable and competent will spread throughout the organization and build your expert power. Non-verbal signals (sounding and looking confident, as discussed in Chapter 2) are also a critical part of developing a reputation as an expert because appearing confident will add to your image of competence.

Expert power is particularly important for those of us who do not necessarily conform to traditional or established conceptions of a leader, for example, women and ethnic minorities (see Chapter 5 for more on the leader prototype). The cultivation of expert and referent power might explain why successful female CEOs are often insiders who have been in the same firm for around thirteen years whereas successful male CEOs are able to come in as outsiders.[6] As women, the female CEOs need strong bases of personal power, built up over time, in order to successfully influence the other members of senior management.

Trust is necessary for exercising social power

Trust is a basic ingredient for any type of upward influence. If the other person does not trust you, why would they do what you request? (Perhaps out of fear, but that is a risky move with someone who has more power and it will definitely damage the relationship). INSEAD business school professor Horacio Falcao offers a definition of trust that teases out its multiple dimensions and makes it more tangible.[7] If you are trying to determine how much influence you might have with someone, ask yourself the following questions to establish how much they trust you:

- **Ability**: Have I demonstrated (to them) the ability to do the job well?
- **Honesty**: Am I transparent and honest with them?
- **Reliability**: Have I delivered on what I promised them?
- **Intimacy**: Do I open up to them?
- **Care for the other person**: Do I show that I care about them?

Use the five questions to figure out which ones are the trust 'pain points' in your relationship and work on building trust in those areas. Most relationships do not require all five dimensions of trust, but the more you have, the stronger the relationship – and the more effective your upward influence will be. Ability, Honesty and Care for the other person are ones that can be worked on immediately by ensuring you perform well and communicate openly and with empathy. Reliability takes longer to establish because it must be proven over time.

Intimacy might not seem relevant to work relationships but in fact it is. It refers to the vulnerability that results from revealing relevant and appropriate personal information. For example, when my father passed away, I had to cancel all my classes and fly to the US for one week. Rather than ask the programme office to send an email telling students I had a 'family emergency', I decided to write and send the email myself. I told my students that I had to fly to the US unexpectedly because my father had passed away from pancreatic cancer, then explained the alternative arrangements that we were making for the classes. The students appreciated my openness and many of them sent me touching condolence emails and cards. Of course, good judgement is required when deciding how much to open up in a work context. When done with sensitivity and good judgement, intimacy can strengthen relationships.

Developing a relationship of trust takes time. Invest the time and effort into cultivating a reputation as someone who is a role model, intelligent and competent, and trustworthy. Then, when you need to exercise upward influence, your reputation 'muscle' will help you make a powerful impact.

How do I find the courage to speak up?

Building your bases of power will give you a platform from which to be heard, but how do you then find the courage to use that platform?

Next I provide five strategies that, when combined, will help you to build your inner power and give you the courage to speak up. These include managing negative emotions, changing your attitude towards failure, using deliberate practice, boosting your self-confidence and generating positive emotions.

• Do not let negative emotions derail you

Many of the times that I silenced my younger self were a result of fear: fear of looking stupid, fear of offending someone, fear of retaliation, fear of wasting others' time and a general fear of drawing attention to myself. Sometimes I was also silenced by a feeling of powerlessness or futility. In other words, negative emotions stopped me from speaking up. Other negative emotions, such as anger, might have the opposite effect, motivating us to act and influence change. But unbridled anger can also cause us to lose perspective and overreact or antagonize others instead of winning them over. If we are to be successful in our upward influence attempts, we must learn to manage our negative emotions.

This is not to say that negative emotions are bad. In fact, they are important signals – they can tell us when something is wrong. When we are motivated to speak up about something, it is often because something has upset us. The challenge is to notice the negative emotions but not let them interfere with our ability to react effectively. Psychologists Kim Gratz and Lizabeth Roemer devised a measure that examines how effectively a person manages their negative emotions.[8] The measure includes six dimensions:

- **Awareness**: How much do I pay attention to how I feel? Do I acknowledge my feelings when I am upset?
- **Clarity**: Can I determine how I am feeling? Can I make sense of my feelings?
- **Acceptance**: When I am upset, can I accept my emotions or do I feel ashamed or weak for feeling that way?
- **Impulse**: Do I have trouble controlling my behaviour when I am upset?
- **Goals**: Do I have trouble getting work done or thinking about other things when I am upset?
- **Strategies**: When I am upset, can I find ways to feel better?

As you might have deduced from the six dimensions, the key to managing negative emotions is not to ignore or stifle them but rather to be aware of them, accept them and devise strategies to make ourselves feel better (talking with friends, for example, or writing in a journal). Ignoring or suppressing negative emotions can reduce our ability to experience positive emotions or increase obsession with negative moods and even depression.[9] At the same time, it is important to control impulsive behaviours (saying or doing something you will regret later) and stay focused on our goals.

TIP: When you are upset, acknowledge and accept the emotion ('I really feel frustrated!') while also controlling any desire to act impulsively (take a deep breath and count to ten). Instead, do something that makes you feel better: call a friend, write in a journal, take a walk, listen to music. Or talk to yourself in the third person ('why is Connson so upset?') and give yourself advice as you would a friend – this not only distances you from the emotion, but also helps you think more clearly about what to do. It might feel strange, but it seems to help (see page 241 for a *Guardian* website article with more details[10]). Negative emotions can be helpful in pointing out the need to act, but only after you have calmed down and thought about them can you decide the best action to take.

TRY THIS: Handling negative emotions with awareness and acceptance

When someone or something upsets you, control the urge to lash back and instead take notice of your own internal turmoil. What are you feeling: is it frustration? Anger?

Despair? Realize that emotion is simply energy and give that ball of energy space to exist. Imagine you have an invisible boundary that is the 'self' and that this boundary is flexible. If you shrink that boundary, the emotional energy has no space and must burst out of you in impulsive actions or words. If you expand that boundary, then the energy becomes just one small part of you and the rest of you remains undisturbed. Get 'bigger' than the emotion. Notice it but do not let it take over.

Another way to think of this is through a metaphor created by a therapist friend of mine.[11] He said to think of your inner self as a kindergarten teacher overseeing many inner children. When one of those children acts up – for example, your angry self or your frustrated self – the teacher (your mature self) hugs that child with love and acceptance. By doing so, the child eventually calms down. If the teacher were to scold the child or push him or her away, or if the child felt judged, the child would only get more upset.

Negative emotions are information given to us in the form of energy. Sometimes the information is pointing to something within us – an insecurity or fear. In such cases we need to be compassionate with ourselves. Sometimes the information is pointing to something in our environment that needs to change. In such cases we might need to engage in upward influence. Once the energy has dissipated, we can figure out what the information was telling us and how to act on that information.

In addition to acknowledging and accepting negative emotions, it can help to cultivate mindfulness. Mindfulness is based on the principles of Buddhist meditation and was first introduced to Western psychology by Jon Kabat-Zinn at the University of Massachusetts Medical School. His Mindfulness-Based Stress Reduction (MBSR) programme is now widely used by therapists and its effectiveness has been demonstrated by researchers. Undergoing mindfulness training can increase awareness and acceptance of our emotions and also make the emotion-generating parts of the brain less reactive.[12] In other words, becoming more mindful can make us less likely to react with such strong emotions.

TRY THIS: Cultivating mindfulness to calm your reactions

The best time to try mindfulness meditation is as soon as you wake up, before your day has started, or just before you go to bed, when your day is over. It does not take much time – 10 minutes is enough to start – but you must ensure you are not disturbed during that time.

1. Find a comfortable place to sit in a semi-cross-legged posture (that is, one leg in front of the other, not on top of each other). I like to sit on my bed or on the floor beside the bed.

2. Place your hands in your lap, palms up, the fingers of one hand over the fingers of the other.

3. Sit up straight and look ahead, then lightly close your eyes. If your body slumps, straighten it slowly and mindfully.

4. Focus on your nostrils and the breath moving in and out of them. Let your thoughts be filled with your breath, thinking 'breathing in', 'breathing out'. When other thoughts enter your mind, let them float away like clouds. If your mind wanders, bring it back to the breath.

5. If you are distracted by sensations in your body, name
   them ('pain, pain, pain' or 'itching, itching, itching')
   until they fade and you can bring your attention back
   to the breath.

Start with ten minutes a day, at least three times a week,
increasing the frequency to every day if you can. You can
even extend the time up to an hour but that is a bigger
time commitment than most people are willing to make, but
with even 10 minutes a day (as I do), over time you should
notice a calming of your mind and its reactions.

• Be persistent and see failure as a learning opportunity

Sometimes we expect to fail in an upward influence attempt – for
example, when we know the committee is unlikely to accept the
proposal, but we want to give it a try anyway. In such situations,
failure is disappointing but not devastating. However, if we are
trying to convince others of what seems to be an obvious solution to
a problem or an obvious issue that needs to be addressed, something
that hardly needs persuasion, and yet the attempt still fails, that
failure can make us question our ability to influence others. In
the introduction to this book, I mentioned when, as a university

student, I tried to convince my parents to let me make my own decisions. This seemed to me such an obviously legitimate request – after all, my friends were allowed to make decisions without deferring to their parents – that I was completely unprepared for my parents' obstinate rejection of the proposal. My reaction to the rejection was to give up on ever trying to influence them again. If I could not convince them of something so obviously correct, my younger self concluded, then I would not be able to convince them of anything at all.

I realize now that my younger self was caught in the trap of the 'fixed mindset': the belief that our abilities and characteristics are fixed at birth. The fixed mindset interprets failure as a reflection of who we are. I failed at convincing my parents, therefore I was a failure as an influencer and there was no point trying again. The alternative to a fixed mindset is a 'growth mindset': the belief that ability is the result of hard work. Psychologist Carol Dweck discovered these two mindsets in her work with children. When given difficult puzzles, some children gave up after a few unsuccessful attempts because failure meant 'I am a failure', while other children were motivated to continue because failure meant 'I haven't learned enough yet'. With a growth mindset, failure is seen as a learning opportunity rather than a traumatic event.[13] Having a growth mindset leads to optimistic self-talk and this optimistic inner voice not only makes a person willing to persevere in the face of adversity, but also motivates them to seek out new challenges which ultimately builds their inner strength and resilience.[14]

> **TIP:** To increase your upward influence skills, cultivate a growth mindset by seeing failures as learning opportunities. If you find yourself thinking 'I am a failure' after a failed attempt, stop and replace this thought with 'I am still learning.'

Every failure is a gift, offering you an opportunity for growth. If you are not sure what you are supposed to learn from a failure, think about it, write about it in your daily journal or talk to a friend or coach. The lessons might not be evident right away – with some of my biggest failures, it took a few years for the pain to dissipate enough for me to see the lesson it held – but the more you accept each failure as a learning experience, the less you will fear failure. And the less you fear failure, the more willing you will be to challenge yourself.

> **TIP:** Take time to reflect on upward influence attempts, both successful and unsuccessful, so you can learn from them. Seek out new opportunities to try upward influence and build your resilience.

• Try again – but deliberately and with different strategies

To build resilience, do not simply try the same thing again and again. Psychologist Anders Ericsson has found that peak performers such as Olympic athletes and world-class musicians engage in 'deliberate practice' rather than mere repetition.[15] That is, they analyse the skill they are trying to learn and establish which components are their weak points, then they work on those specific components. A musician who finds herself stumbling on a particular set of chords will work only on those chords for the next few practice sessions until they flow easily.

> **TIP:** Try to determine which elements of upward influence are your weak points. Do you sound hesitant? Do you look unsure of yourself? Is your opening argument weak? Do you have trouble establishing rapport? Are you unable to quickly think of responses to the other person's concerns? Work on those specific elements before making another upward influence attempt.

Don't just get better – get creative. Think of more than one way of reaching the same goal. This will give you a back-up plan if your first strategy doesn't work. As Ericsson explains, in order to improve a skill, 'generally the solution is not "try harder" but rather "try differently".[16]

> **TIP:** Adjust your strategy if it doesn't work the first
> time. Instead of banging your head against the wall,
> find a way to climb over that wall. If you get flustered
> every time you walk into your boss's office, try inviting
> your boss for coffee outside of the office where you
> might feel more relaxed. If your boss did not seem
> interested in your idea the first time, find out what
> their interests and concerns are so that you can
> re-think and re-frame the idea.

• Grow your confidence from the inside out

In presentation skills training, we are often told to 'fake it till you make it' – in other words, look confident on the outside and you will eventually feel confident on the inside. But this can take years, and those who are particularly low in self-confidence might give up before any shift happens. Engaging in upward influence can create an even bigger challenge for our shaky self-confidence because of the power difference. In fact, psychologist Dacher Keltner and his colleagues at the University of California at Berkeley discovered that in interactions where both parties perceive unequal power (boss–employee, teacher–student or even older–younger or male–

female), awareness of the power difference can affect the behaviours and emotions of both people. The person with less power tends to feel inhibited, second-guessing their actions and worrying about displeasing the other person. The person with more power tends to feel disinhibited, engaging in more spontaneous actions and focusing only on what they want, not how it might affect others.[17] The disinhibition of having more power might explain why some bosses abuse their position and the inhibition of having less power might explain why some employees hesitate to speak up.

> **TIP:** When engaging in upward influence, try to avoid thinking about the power difference between you and the other person. Instead of your relationship ('this is my boss'), remind yourself of their role in helping you achieve your goal ('this is the person who can implement the policy I am proposing'). Stay focused on your goal to avoid thinking about the power difference and being inhibited by it.

When psychologists run experiments on power and influence, they need to make study participants feel instantly more or less powerful. A widely used method for doing this is a short, ten-minute writing exercise in which participants are asked to describe a time when they had power over others (controlling the ability of the other person to get what they wanted, for example) or a time when others had that same power over them.[18] Writing for ten minutes about this time is enough to trigger feelings of high or low power that then affect their subsequent behaviour, such as (for high-power participants) taking more cookies from a shared plate or taking the initiative in an experiment to move an annoying electric fan. Participants engaging in the high-power writing exercise also reported greater feelings of control, optimism and confidence afterwards.

The high-power writing exercise has helped participants do better in mock job applications and mock interviews for admission to business school.[19] The participants which the judges were more likely to hire turned out to be the ones who had recalled the high-power incident because they expressed more self-confidence in their letters. They were also more successful in the 15-minute mock admission interviews. The interviewers accepted 68 per cent of the candidates from the high-power group, 47 per cent from a control group (who did not do any writing exercise) and only 26 per cent from the low-power group. Even though participants did not suspect any connection between the writing exercise and the subsequent task (they were told it was an exercise for handwriting analysis), the ones who recalled the high-power incident somehow ended up being perceived as being more confident and persuasive.

TRY THIS: Recalling past experiences to boost feelings of confidence

Get a piece of paper, set a timer and spend ten minutes recalling and writing about an incident in which you felt powerful or in control. Maybe you were the one who chose the party venue that everyone loved or you complained about the service and managed to get an apology or you changed a process at work that resulted in greater efficiency. Write about the details of the incident and how it made you feel.

Exercising control over your job and your life, even in small ways, will help you develop a feeling of personal power. And reflecting on those incidents on a daily basis will amplify their effects on your overall sense of power and feeling of confidence.

In order to gain a temporary boost of confidence, try 'power posing'. This idea was popularized by psychologist Amy Cuddy in her 2012 TED Talk.[20] The video has attracted more than 50 million views and has also sparked criticism and controversy because other researchers were unable to replicate all of the original results. The TED Talk is based on research conducted by Dana Carney, Amy Cuddy and

Andy Yap in which they found that holding 'power poses' (standing with your legs apart to make the letter 'A' and with hands on your hips or raised above your head) for a total of two minutes resulted in lower cortisol levels (less stress), higher testosterone levels (more risk-taking) and greater feelings of power.[21] Subsequent research was unable to replicate the changes in hormone levels – but it *did* replicate the increase in feelings of power.[22]

Not only that, but power posing also improved others' perceptions of participants giving a five-minute job interview speech detailing their strengths and qualifications for their dream job. Independent judges who did not know whether or not participants had held a power pose before their speech watched the recordings of the speeches and found half the participants to be more hireable because their speeches were significantly more captivating and conveyed more confidence and enthusiasm. They were, as you might have guessed, those who had held the power poses beforehand.[23] It seems the effect of power posing is similar to that of the writing exercise. It did not affect anything concrete such as participants' posture while giving the speech, but it did make the power-posing participants somehow appear more engaging and confident.

> **TIP:** For an extra boost of confidence before an important interview or big presentation, go to the bathroom and hold a power pose for two minutes.

When I do this, I take a wide-legged stance and raise
my arms in the air for two minutes, take a few deep
breaths, and imagine a white light shining through
me towards my audience. This light represents the
message I am going to deliver and focuses me on my
goal rather than my nervousness.

• Be someone that others want to be around

Have you ever met someone who has such a positive energy that you
want to be around them as much as possible? Like moths drawn to
a flame, we are often attracted to people who make us feel happy
and optimistic. Being such a person could be a source of referent
power, making others want to work with you and listen to you. The
key is to balance the two types of happiness: 'eudaimonia', which is
based on having meaning and purpose in life, and 'hedonia', which
is based on pleasure. Having a feeling of purpose can give you a
positive energy that is contagious, making others want to work with
you and boosting your referent power. We often spend too much
time on hedonic pleasures, such as drinking with friends or binge-
watching TV shows, and not enough time on eudaimonic activities
such as volunteering at a local charity or running a marathon. This is
probably because eudaimonic activities are not always pleasurable in
the short term, but they provide a more enduring long-term benefit
to our well-being than hedonic activities.[24] In fact, in older adults,

higher levels of purpose in life are associated with better cognitive functioning, reduced risk of stroke and less disrupted sleep.[25]

> **TIP:** When planning your free time, plan eudaimonic activities (such as learning a new skill or helping others) in addition to hedonic activities (like going on holiday or watching a movie).

Just as importantly, find a sense of meaning and purpose at work. This might involve adjusting your responsibilities – or adjusting the way you think about those responsibilities. Follow the example of the fabled hospital caretaker who defined his job not as 'cleaning the bathrooms' but as 'helping the patients recover'. Getting to know some of the people who benefit from your work can help you feel that sense of purpose. University fundraisers who were shown letters written by scholarship students explaining how they benefited from the money raised were so motivated by the students' stories that they more than doubled the amount of money they raised in the following weeks. Fundraisers who had instead been given letters written by former fundraisers explaining how fundraising had helped their career prospects did not show any change in money raised.[26] We want to feel that we are making a difference to someone, that we matter. Find a way to help yourself see the difference you are making and generate that feeling of meaning and purpose.

> **TIP:** Think about your work and how it benefits others. Get to know some of the people who benefit from your work. If the beneficiaries are not obvious, change the way you think about your work. The stonemason who sees his job as 'building a cathedral' has a greater sense of purpose than one who sees his job as 'cutting blocks of stone'.

Connecting to your creative side can also generate positive energy and a feeling of purpose, making you someone that others want to be around. Julia Cameron, playwright, novelist, songwriter and poet, argues that all humans have the urge to create and by fulfilling that urge we bring meaning to our lives. She defines creativity as a sense of fun and openness that many of us have lost in adulthood. Cameron's book, *The Artist's Way*, offers a twelve-week course designed to help readers recover that sense of fun and get back in touch with their creative self.[27] A friend gave me this book when I was in my mid-thirties in Hong Kong. If I had known about eudaimonia and hedonia back then, I would have said that I did too many hedonic activities and not enough eudaimonic activities. I no longer felt a sense of personal growth at work and I had lost sight of my purpose in life. While *The Artist's Way* did not show me my purpose, it did boost my positive emotions and helped me understand myself better. The 'morning pages' – a stream-of-consciousness daily writing exercise – increased my awareness of those things in my life that were blocking me. The weekly 'artist date' – a two-hour fun activity to be done by yourself – brought a forgotten sense of fun and adventure into my life. Ultimately, the book made me emotionally and psychologically more open to the changes that I was to make only one year later: moving to California to study for a PhD and start a new career in academia.

> **TIP:** Creativity is a eudaimonic activity that can boost your sense of purpose in life. Introduce it in a way that works for you. This could mean wandering around art galleries, dancing to music in your living room or inviting friends around for an arts-and-crafts session. Rediscover the joy and fun of being alive, and boost your referent power, making yourself someone that others want to be around.

You have learned how to use power bases to build a platform from which to be noticed and heard, and how to manage negative emotions, develop self-confidence and resilience, and generate a sense of joy and purpose in life. But there is one more internal barrier to being influential: that voice inside your head. The one that keeps whispering you're not good enough and won't be able to make a difference. So let's find out how to control that voice inside your head.

CHAPTER 4

Control the Voice Inside Your Head

Daniel had recently been promoted to be head of his department at work and arrived at the strategy meeting feeling nervous. He looked around at the other senior leaders and wondered how he had got there – they all seemed so much more polished and experienced than he was. During the meeting, he kept being distracted by the thought that his promotion must have been a fluke. As the afternoon wore on, he felt increasingly overwhelmed by the fast-paced discussion. This was a big mistake, he thought. I'm not ready for this.

Carol couldn't believe what a disaster the presentation had been. She had carefully prepared a highly technical presentation for the client and knew her numbers inside and out. But, as she was setting up in the meeting room, one of the attendees arrived, sat down, and asked her for a cup of tea. She awkwardly explained that she was the presenter and he apologized profusely, but the damage was done. She was suddenly acutely aware of being a lone woman presenting to a room of men and, despite weeks of preparation, she stumbled over the numbers and even managed to get some of them mixed up.

Daniel and Carol are victims of the undermining beliefs that reside inside our heads and are triggered by certain situations. While many of the situations I portray in this book occur in the workplace, these concepts apply to situations outside the workplace as well, including at school, at home and in your community. Any time you want to exercise upward influence, that voice inside your head can undermine you.

But the voice inside your head is not all bad. Like emotions, which can hinder or help you reach your goals, the voice inside your head can also hinder or help. By learning to control this voice, you ensure that it is more helpful than harmful. The previous chapter gave you tips on managing your emotions and there is a strong link between thoughts and emotions. A negative emotion (fear) can trigger an undermining belief ('I can't do this') – or vice versa – and the two reinforce each other in a vicious circle. So, the more you learn to manage your negative emotions, the easier it will be to control the undermining thoughts. And the more you generate positive emotions, the easier it will be to generate encouraging thoughts.

In this chapter, we focus on the thoughts themselves – the voice inside your head. I start by examining three types of belief that could undermine your ability to be influential: beliefs about your success, status and impact. These beliefs operate subconsciously, therefore becoming aware of them can help you manage them. Then I share a strategy for creating a helpful voice inside your head through the use of positive 'triggers'. Finally, I explore the stages of psychological development and how this affects the way we approach upward influence.

Undermining beliefs about success: 'I don't deserve to be here'

Daniel's experience as head of division is an example of impostor syndrome (or impostor phenomenon) in which a person feels their success is not deserved. People who suffer from impostor syndrome are convinced their success comes from luck rather than actual ability, that their accomplishments are not as impressive as others' and should be discounted and that they are fooling everyone.[1] In other words, they feel like an impostor.

Clinical psychologists Pauline Clance and Suzanne Imes first discovered this phenomenon among high-achieving women in their clinical practice – women who had PhDs and academic jobs but were nonetheless convinced they were not intelligent and had deceived those around them.[2] Other researchers have since found that men are just as likely to feel like impostors.[3] If you want to find out if you suffer from impostor syndrome, visit Pauline Clance's website where she shares a copy of her Impostor Phenomenon test (for personal use only).[4]

Research on impostor syndrome has found that people who feel like impostors do not necessarily perform their jobs worse than non-impostors, but they are less likely to engage in extra activities that benefit the organization and fall outside their role expectations, such as serving on a cross-functional committee or organizing a social event. This is because impostors also tend to suffer from anxiety, low self-esteem, excessive perfectionism (having unreasonably high expectations of oneself) and low self-efficacy (the belief that one is able to achieve one's goals).[5]

One of the ways that Clance and Imes helped their clients overcome their feelings of being impostors was by engaging them in group therapy with other people experiencing impostor syndrome. On hearing other people who were clearly successful also claim to be impostors, the clients noticed how improbable their own impostor beliefs were. Clients were also encouraged to keep a record of positive feedback and notice how they prevented themselves from accepting that feedback. For example, if they read a piece of positive feedback and found themselves denying it, they should notice that they were doing so.[6]

TIP: Find others who suffer from impostor syndrome and each talk about your achievements. Notice how the others undermine themselves by discounting impressive achievements and attributing their success to luck. Then notice how you do the same. Help each other see how capable you all are and how you are all undermining your confidence unnecessarily. Validate each other's achievements and help each other feel ownership for successes.

TRY THIS: Creating a 'Smile File' of positive feedback

Create a folder – electronic or paper – in which you gather all the meaningful positive feedback that you receive. This is your 'Smile File'. Whenever a piece of feedback makes you smile and feel like you made an impact, keep a copy of it. This includes emails, cards, photos and anything else that reminds you of the positive impact you have had on others. If the feedback is spoken, type it up and keep a copy.

Read through the contents of the folder every once in a while, and especially when starting a new role or job, as that's when we most often need a confidence boost. Notice if you are discounting or denying any of the feedback ('it wasn't that difficult', 'I didn't contribute as much as the others'). When you notice this, stop yourself. Replace those thoughts with ones that acknowledge the feedback ('that was a lot of hard work', 'I really made a difference'). These are your accomplishments. Own them and be proud of them.

Impostor syndrome is associated with success. The more successful you become and the more recognized you are, the more susceptible you may be to feeling like an impostor. You might not have full-blown impostor syndrome, but often it is difficult to silence those doubting voices. I was recently invited to speak at a major conference and, when I saw the list of other speakers, the voice inside my head started whispering impostor-like thoughts: 'Did they make a mistake inviting me?', 'Do they realize how little I know compared with the others?' But I knew better than to let those thoughts spiral out of control. Instead, I reminded myself of the positive feedback that I had received from previous audiences and replaced the voice in my head with messages about the benefits I would bring this audience: 'They need to hear what I am going to say', 'They will learn a lot from me'. I have found that messages focused on others, such as these, are far more effective than messages focused on myself. If I tried to give myself a pep talk such as 'you're great at this!', my inner self would be cynically rolling her eyes. Instead, when I focus on benefiting others, the desire to help can drown out the doubting voices in my head.

> **TIP:** When impostor-like thoughts prevent you from engaging in upward influence, replace them with thoughts about your goal and the benefits you are creating by raising the issue or making the suggestion (see my example above and Daniel's example below). Focus on that goal and the people who will benefit from your efforts.

What advice would I give Daniel to overcome his own impostor syndrome? First of all, Daniel needs to remember that taking on a new role is always challenging and the feeling of being overwhelmed does not mean he is not qualified – it simply means he is new. If he hadn't been so distracted by his own negative thoughts, he wouldn't have found the discussion so difficult to follow. Daniel should replace his negative thoughts with positive ones (if he simply told himself not to have the negative thought, he would focus on it more – it's like being told 'do not think about a white bear'). Daniel can get a much-needed confidence boost by thinking about what he brings to the role and the benefits he hopes to create for his team and the organization. Creating a few one-liners to summarize those benefits can help turn around his negative thoughts. For example, whenever he thinks 'I don't deserve to be here', he should immediately remind himself that 'I am creating a more inclusive environment for my team.' This reminds him that he is needed and is bringing value, and it should help strengthen his resolve to stick with it and do a good job.

Undermining beliefs about status: 'I am not as good as everyone else'

Carol's disastrous presentation is an example of stereotype threat, when a negative stereotype threatens our self-confidence and performance. By being reminded of her identity as a woman, Carol was subconsciously reminded of the stereotypical belief that women are worse at maths than men. True to the stereotype, she then performed worse. Stereotype threat was discovered by social psychologists Claude Steele and Joshua Aronson, who examined the effect on undergraduate African American students of the erroneous belief that African Americans are less intelligent than white Americans.[7] Steele and Aronson argued that African Americans do not need to believe this racist stereotype – they only need to know that it exists for it to affect their performance.

Stereotype threat occurs in a specific type of situation: when faced with a difficult task where your skills are being evaluated (a test or interview, for example). In Steele and Aronson's original study, students were given a test comprised of difficult items from the verbal section of the Graduate Record Examinations (GRE), a standardized test used for entry into graduate school. When students were told the test was simply a problem-solving test that did not reflect intellectual ability, the black students performed as well as the white students. However, when they were told that the test was to assess intellectual ability, the black students performed worse than the white students – and worse than the black students who thought it was a problem-solving test.

Similarly in Carol's case, her presentation was a chance for the client to evaluate her abilities as a consultant. If the presentation had not been so highly technical, she probably would have done a great job despite having been reminded of her gender. In fact, she might have thought 'I'll show them what a woman can do!' and performed better than usual. This is what researchers found when they studied gender in negotiations. When women are told that the negotiation assesses their ability, they tend to encounter stereotype threat and perform worse than men. But when women and men are reminded of how to succeed (that is, effective negotiators are rational and assertive), then women perform better than men.[8] Stereotype threat only impairs performance when the task is really difficult. The difficulty of the task raises self-doubt ('why am I finding this so hard?'), which reminds them of the negative stereotype and distracts them from the task at hand.[9]

TIP: If you are engaging in a task that is challenging for you, you might be susceptible to stereotype threat. To counteract this, practise the task in a safe environment so that you feel confident when placed in a more threatening context (for example, practise negotiating in an all-female environment first). If this is not possible, see the other tips in this section.

Negative stereotypes can be activated by being one of very few women or ethnic minorities in the room. Being a 'solo' (the only woman or minority) or 'token' (less than 20 per cent representation in the group) results in self-consciousness that can affect our ability to think and perform.[10] Growing up in suburban United States, I was often the only non-white (and non-blonde) person in the room. As a child, I did not think about the fact that I looked different – we do not walk around with a mirror in front of us all day – and of course I did not feel different because I had been born there. But my differences were pointed out to me repeatedly by other children ('Chinese, Japanese, dirty knees, look at these!'), in adulthood by random strangers ('go back to where you come from!'), and in more polite ways by new acquaintances ('where are you from?', 'your English is really good!'). When it happens often enough, it becomes part of your identity and the way you relate to the world. Psychologists call it 'stigma consciousness': being conscious of the stigma of being different. People who are high in stigma consciousness are more sensitive to the possibility of being stereotyped and discriminated against and, because their stigmatized identity is always at the top of their mind, they are also more likely to experience stereotype threat.[11]

As a young adult, I had not heard of stigma consciousness, but I knew what it felt like. Whenever I was the only non-white person in the room, I suddenly felt awkward and self-conscious. Being the 'solo' made me feel powerless, triggered negative emotions and inhibited my behaviour. It is no wonder I had trouble making my voice heard when I was younger – much of the time I was silencing it myself! Stigma consciousness will vary by individual, and I noticed mine seemed high compared to my Chinese-American friends who had grown up in areas with a larger Chinese-American population. Many of them did not seem stigma conscious at all. Context does have a big impact, though there are individual differences as well. My sister, who grew up in the same context as I did, was less stigma conscious than I was – perhaps because, as the older sister, I shielded her from some of the racism or maybe her extroverted personality protected her by surrounding her with many friends.

Can stigma consciousness be reduced? Someone who is stigma conscious feels like an outsider because of their stigmatized identity (gender, ethnicity, sexuality, religion, class and so on). To counteract this, it can help to feel like an integral part of the community. Hispanic and black university students who were randomly assigned to a fixed schedule where they took classes with the same set of students (of all ethnicities) developed a sense of community that boosted their morale and academic performance.[12] Belonging to a close-knit team or club could have the same effect. Or, in my case, a sense of belonging to a family: when I hang out with my husband and his extended family, I am often the only non-white person in the room, but the feeling of warmth and acceptance is so strong that it eliminates any possibility of stigma consciousness. Moving to Hong Kong in my late twenties also helped turn things around for me. For the first time, I was surrounded by people who looked like me – not just on the street where I could blend in with the crowd (what a relief!), but even on TV and in newspapers and magazines. I began to appreciate my facial features and Chinese heritage. At the same time, I was growing older, more mature and less self-conscious in general. Instead of obsessing about my ethnic identity, I learned to focus on my career and personal goals.

> **TIP:** Find a community to which you feel a strong sense of belonging based on shared interests or values. To reduce stigma consciousness, the community must be diverse. If it is comprised only of others who look like you, it could exacerbate the feeling of stigma consciousness as the whole group feels like outsiders.

We all have multiple identities – something that makes us all potentially susceptible to stereotype threat. While most stereotypes disadvantage women or ethnic minorities, even a white man might find himself in a situation that sparks self-doubts, which affect his performance, for example, if he is among other white men and he is the youngest, the shortest or the only one from a working-class background. But stereotypes can also be positive, giving us a 'stereotype lift' that helps us perform better. Social psychologist Margaret Shih and colleagues demonstrated this in a study using female Asian-American university students in the US, testing two opposing stereotypes: that women have poor quantitative skills and Asians (for example, Chinese) have excellent quantitative skills.[13] Before taking a difficult maths test, students were asked to fill out a questionnaire about residential life at the university that focused on their gender identity (for example, do you prefer single-sex or co-ed housing?), ethnic identity (for example, how many generations have your family lived in America?), or neither (for example, do you live on campus?). They then took the difficult maths test. Students in all three groups were female Asian-American undergraduates, yet their performance differed significantly depending on which identity had been triggered. Those reminded of their gender performed the worst and those reminded of their ethnicity performed the best, even out-performing the control group. Stereotypes can help us perform better or worse, depending on the identity being triggered.

TIP: If you find yourself in a situation where stereotype threat is likely, think about how to counteract it by focusing on a positive stereotype or a different part of your identity. For example, the woman in a male-dominated environment could give herself a stereotype lift by reminding herself of the stereotypical belief that women are better at emotional intelligence or relationship building than men.

What advice would I have given Carol if I had been in the presentation with her? As soon as she noticed that she was feeling unsure of herself, she should have gone to the bathroom for a short break, holding a power pose while focusing on a part of her identity that was not susceptible to stereotype threat. For example, she could have reminded herself of her identity as an alumna of a prestigious university, as the winner of an award at work last year or of her previous job as a statistician. Any of those would have helped her regain confidence in that situation. By filling her mind with that identity and doing a power pose, she should have been able to return to the meeting room with more confidence.

Undermining beliefs about impact: 'I can't make a difference anyway'

Marilyn couldn't believe it when she heard the youth activity centre in her neighbourhood was going to close next year. It had been a critical part of her own life when her children were teenagers many years ago, giving them a safe place to go after school. Where would the kids go now? She called her friends to complain and they agreed it was a catastrophe. Finally, one friend said, 'Why don't you do something about it?' But Marilyn laughed at the idea that anyone would listen to her. She wouldn't even know where to start. Besides, she was used to bad things happening and had accepted that life was full of disappointments.

The locus of control is one of the most widely studied personality traits and examines our beliefs about whether events are controlled internally (by the person themselves) or externally (by forces outside their control such as other people, chance or luck).[14] Internal and external locus of control are two ends of a scale and there is a great deal of variation along that scale. Generally, it is better to fall towards the 'internal' end of the scale, believing that you have control over the outcomes in your life. People with an internal locus of control tend to be high achievers who can recover from negative events. In contrast, those who fall towards the 'external' end of the scale believe there is little or nothing they can do to change their situation, that their efforts will not result in the desired outcome or even that their behaviour is not self-determined (that is, they had no choice but to behave that way).

Locus of control is a personality trait, making it something that does not easily change. But regardless of your locus of control, you can use Stephen Covey's 'Circle of Concern and Circle of Influence' to increase the sense of control over your life.[15] Our Circle of Concern is large and contains those things that we care about, such as our family, finances, health, the economy, the climate and so on. Our Circle of Influence is much smaller and contains only the subset of things within our Circle of Concern that we can control or influence, such as our behaviour, our work and our attitude. People who focus primarily on their Circle of Concern are 'reactive': they merely react to the events around them, complaining, blaming and feeling victimized. People who focus primarily on their Circle of Influence are 'proactive': rather than complaining, they think about what they can do to influence events in a positive way. These two circles give us a more flexible way of thinking about the world and our impact in it because we can shift our focus from one circle to the other. If we think of ourselves as 'someone with an external locus of control', there is not much we can do about it since it is a personality trait. But if we think of ourselves as 'someone who focuses mostly on our Circle of Concern', a solution becomes more clear: we can shift our efforts into our Circle of Influence.

TRY THIS: Growing your Circle of Influence

To be more influential, you must believe that you can make a difference. Mapping out your Circle of Concern (things you are concerned about) and Circle of Influence (actions you can take) can help convince you that you can make an impact. On a piece of paper, draw a line down the middle creating two columns. Label the first column 'Concerns' and the second column 'Actions'.

- In the first column, make a list of the things that you are unhappy about or are worrying about. This could include issues from your work life, personal life or health. This should not be an endless list of complaints, but rather a list of those things that are weighing the most heavily on your mind.

- In the second column, think of an action you can take for each of your concerns. This does not have to be a solution to the problem, but simply an action that brings you closer to resolving it. For example, if you are upset about a new policy at work, you could speak to someone involved with the policy to find out more about the thinking behind it. If you are worried about your teenager's phone usage, you could schedule a time to talk to them about how to limit that usage. In all cases, try to understand the situation from the other person's point of view before taking further action.

Think creatively about actions you can take. Sometimes the best action might be 'stop worrying about this', which is what I did when I realized that life is too short to count calories. The action that I took for the concern 'I need to lose 15 pounds because my suits don't fit' was 'get my suits altered and stop worrying about my weight'. By engaging in this exercise, you may be surprised at how long your list of actions turns out to be (that is, how big your Circle of Influence is) and how much control you have over your life.

Do not misunderstand me: I am not suggesting that we become control freaks. There is a difference between the Circle of Influence and the need for obsessive control. The former is a healthy attitude towards the parts of our lives that bother us. The latter is an unhealthy desire to control people and events and eliminate uncertainty. We cannot eliminate uncertainty and we cannot control the people around us. We can only influence them and then accept the outcome.

Even if something is within our Circle of Influence, we are not always able to influence it perfectly. Giving instructions to someone else is within your control, but you cannot control whether they follow those instructions correctly. Carol's presentation was within her Circle of Influence, yet it did not go well. At times like that, the one thing we can control is our attitude. We can choose to accept and deal with it rather than wallow in denial or self-pity. The time you spend thinking, 'why me? Why do I deserve this?' could be spent more productively (and less stressfully!) thinking, 'okay, this has happened. Now what can I do to fix it?' When I work with students who have failed an assessment, I notice the ones who do best – emotionally and academically – are the ones who are able to move quickly past the knee-jerk response 'this is so unfair!' to acceptance of the failure. Only then are they able to ask, 'what went wrong and what do I need to do differently?' The more we can accept life as it is, rather than complaining about it, the more energy we will have to focus on making it even better. Complaining gives energy to our negative emotions without any hope of resolution, making us feel powerless. Sometimes commiserating with someone who has suffered the same as us can help us feel better. But notice when the commiserating turns into stoking the fires of discontent with no resolution. At that point, make a conscious decision to either act on the problem or let it go.

TIP: When something goes wrong (a failed exam or cancelled flight), it can trigger two reactions: a

negative emotion (being upset) as well as resistance
(denial). Notice that resistance and treat it as any
other negative emotion (see the 'Handling Negative
Emotions' exercise in Chapter 3, page 91), letting
the energy dissipate naturally. You could even try
to notice where you feel the resistance in your
body (tension in your shoulders, for example) and
consciously relax it. When the emotional energy has
dissipated enough for you to think clearly, decide
what to do about the situation.

What if you have been trying to change a situation and have
failed repeatedly? Or if there is nothing you can do to change the
situation? You still have one thing you can influence: your attitude.
As Maya Angelou said, 'If you don't like something, change it. If
you can't change it, change your attitude.'[16] This does not mean
giving up – quite the opposite. It means we must make the best of
the situation and, perhaps by changing our attitude, the situation
will eventually change as well. If you have a difficult boss, you
might not be able to change their behaviour, but you can manage
your own attitude and behaviour. Instead of seeing the boss's bad-
tempered criticism as personal attacks, see it as feedback with
which to improve future relations. Instead of complaining about
the boss's micro-managing style, focus on being transparent and

reliable and build a relationship of trust that might eventually soften the micro-managing behaviour.

What advice would I give Marilyn about the imminent closing of the youth activity centre? Marilyn should start by mapping her Circle of Concern and Circle of Influence as described above. This will convince her that she is not helpless. Then, to tackle this specific challenge, she should find out more about community activism at her local library or community centre. When trying to influence policy change, additional support is usually needed and she might find a community group that is willing to take up the cause. If not, she can sit down with her friends and brainstorm a list of possible actions, for example, contacting her local councillor or creating a petition. She can then decide which actions she is most comfortable taking and start with those. If she can get her friends to help, even better.

Marilyn could also read Gina Martin's book *Be the Change: A toolkit for the activist in you.*[17] Martin is an ordinary citizen who was so enraged when a man took a photo up her skirt at a music festival and the police said they could not do anything about it, that she campaigned to have such acts of 'upskirting' made illegal. The book provides guidance and resources for citizens who want to change a policy or law (within the UK political system).

When we focus on our Circle of Influence, we might be surprised at how large it actually is – it might even be the first time we realize we have one. The next time you find yourself complaining about things in your Circle of Concern, make yourself consider the actions you can take for each of those concerns. The more we live our lives within our Circle of Influence, the larger that influence becomes.

Creating positive voices in your head

I once sat in on a workshop run by a friend of mine who has a background in acting and directing and watched him use an unusual technique to help executives improve their influence style.[18] He asked each manager in the workshop to role-play an issue they were having with one of their team members (the team member was played by another manager). He said he would stop the role play at some point and give the manager a slip of paper with a sentence that he called a 'trigger'. The manager was instructed to think about the trigger, then replay the role play with that trigger in mind.

One manager role-played a conversation with a team member who was working from home. The manager was convinced the team member was not actually doing much work at home and wanted him to start working from the office again. The initial conversation became heated very quickly and it was clear that neither person was listening to the other. My friend stopped the role play, wrote down a 'trigger', gave it to the manager and told him to try again. In the second version, it felt like the manager was a different person. He was concerned and compassionate, resulting in a much more productive conversation. Afterwards, he revealed the trigger was 'you are my long lost brother and I love you'.

Another manager said one of her team members refused to participate in team-building activities because he felt they were a waste of time. The initial role play did not go well. The manager was trying to be understanding while also requesting the team member to participate, but the team member simply refused. My friend again stopped the role play and provided a 'trigger'. Again, it felt like the manager was transformed into a different person. She was assertive, strong and in control, and the team member soon acquiesced. The trigger? 'I just bought this company and you're fired.'

While these triggers are amusing and perhaps more dramatic than you might use in a normal situation, they illustrate an important point: that changing the voice in our heads can change the way we influence others. The managers in the workshop had no acting experience and yet, when given a new statement for that voice in their heads, they made an immediate and seamless transformation. The key is finding a trigger that changes your feelings or assumptions about the situation or person. The first manager changed from seeing their team member as a bad person who was trying to cheat the company to seeing him as a good person whom he cared about. The second manager changed from seeing the situation as one in which she should motivate and engage the team member to one where she should take control and command him.

TRY THIS: Writing positive statements for the voice in your head

Take a piece of paper and divide it into three columns. Label the first column 'Situation', the second 'Old Trigger', and the third 'New Trigger'.

Situation: Think about a recent interaction that went badly or an upcoming interaction that you fear might go badly. Perhaps there is a difficult conversation that you need to have or there might be a skill you are trying to develop.

Old Trigger: Write down what you think the voice in your head was (or is) saying that is not helpful. Imagine yourself in the situation, feel what it is like and then listen to the words behind the feelings – the assumptions that you are making about the situation, yourself or the other person. Try to identify the one statement or assumption that is at the core of the situation.

New Trigger: Write down the new statement that you think would be more helpful in that situation. This involves flipping the old trigger into a new, more helpful, version. Notice the change in feelings that come with the new trigger. If there is no change in feeling, rewrite the trigger into something stronger.

Situation	Old Trigger	New Trigger
Carol might write: 'highly technical client presentations'.	'Technical presentations are scary.'	'Technical presentations showcase my skills as a statistician' and the feeling created is pride.
Daniel might write: 'senior strategy meetings'.	'I'm the least experienced person in the room.'	'I bring a fresh perspective to the group' and the feeling created is value.
A frustrated parent might write: 'talking to my teenager about reducing phone usage'.	'My teenager is incapable of self-control.'	'My teenager is a sensible person who needs some support' and the feeling created is trust.

Role-play the situation with a friend or colleague both with and without the new trigger and get feedback. When you identify a new trigger that helps, keep it somewhere easily accessible so that you remember to use it. By changing your perception of a situation or person, you change your ability to influence them.

Finding the guiding voice in your head

After working in Hong Kong as a management consultant for a few years, I turned thirty and felt the need to make a change in my life. My internal guiding voice told me that getting an MBA was the best next step. So I started to fill out applications. At one point, I had to write to a former employer asking for a letter of recommendation. In a moment of clarity, as I was explaining to her why I wanted to pursue an MBA, I realized it was because all the senior consultants had one and I wanted to be as respected as they were. In fact, if I was honest with myself, I did not enjoy management consulting at all – I only enjoyed the parts of my job where I was training new consultants. I stopped filling out MBA applications and started looking for a job as a training manager.

The first step to being influential is deciding when upward influence is necessary – and it is our internal guiding voice that helps us decide. But sometimes that internal guide is not fully developed. Why did my internal guide tell me to get an MBA when it was the wrong thing for me? Because at that stage in my life, my internal guide was reflecting the voices around me. I had not yet developed my own view of the world and was instead seeing the world through other people's eyes. Since the consultants around me valued the MBA qualification (as did my parents), I internalized that and believed it was what I valued as well. My ability to break away from those external voices marked my transition to the next stage of development.

Harvard psychologist Robert Kegan identified five stages of human development that represent different ways of understanding the world.[19] The first stage is childhood where the world is a magical place that we cannot fully grasp. The second stage, which I will call *egotistical*, is adolescence and young adulthood where we see the world only through the lens of our own wants and needs. In the third stage, *other-focused*, we see the world through others' eyes. In the fourth stage, *principled*, we develop our own independent view of the world. Kegan did not find anyone who had reached the fifth stage,[20] when we are able to transcend our individual world view, holding many view points at the same time and being comfortable with shades of grey, so I will not cover it here.

Most adults find themselves in stages two (*egotistical*), three (*other-focused*), or four (*principled*) – or in the transition between those stages. The transition is slow and could take years or decades, and some people might stay at the same stage for most of their lives. While each stage is more complex than the one before, that does not mean it is necessarily 'better'. These stages do not differentiate in terms of morality or intelligence – they primarily differ in how we make sense of the world, especially in our ability to take other people's perspectives and handle complex situations.

Movement from one stage to the next requires a combination of challenge and support. At the age of thirty, I was in the other-focused stage. By deciding to break away from the voices around me,

I was forcing myself to move to the principled stage. In my case, the challenge was deciding to do my own thing. This was different from my adolescent phase of 'doing my own thing' when I chose the opposite of what my parents wanted in order to prove my independence. With this decision, I was not trying to prove anything to anyone. I was learning from my experience of training consultants and the realization that it was something I enjoyed and was good at. The support was reading self-help books to determine what I truly believed, finding friends who supported me in my decision and making sure I did not quit my old job before finding a new one. In the transition to the principled stage, I started to create a set of personal principles with which to guide myself and that took another decade to fully develop.

How is this relevant to upward influence? The stage at which you find yourself will affect your approach to upward influence and the stage of development of the person you want to influence will determine how they react to your influence attempt. Here I provide more detail on stages two through to four and how they might affect upward influence (stage 1 is childhood which is not relevant here).

• Stage 2 (egotistical): *Seeing the world through your own needs and wants*

Someone at the egotistical stage of development has not yet developed the ability to see the world through the eyes of others.

They understand that other people have needs and desires, but they are unable to hold their own perspective and others' perspectives in their mind at the same time. As a result, they are unable to truly empathize with others, especially when others get in the way of their own desires. This is a natural developmental phase for children and adolescents, but some adults can also be found here. Kegan found around 1 in 10 adults (aged 19 to 55) remained at the egotistical stage and another 2 out of 10 were in the transition phase from egotistical to other-focused.[21]

People who are at the egotistical stage of development will speak up only when their interests are at stake and will propose solutions that benefit themselves.

> **TIP:** If you are trying to influence someone who is at the egotistical stage, your arguments should focus on that person and their interests. The more you can understand their needs and wants, the more convincing you will be. If they can see personal benefit in your proposal, they are more likely to support it.

• Stage 3 (other-focused): *Seeing the world through others' eyes*

People at the other-focused stage have internalized one or more value systems, such as a national culture, organizational culture or religious or political beliefs. They have learned to prioritize those values over their own needs and desires. They are able to see the world from the perspectives of others and reflect on the impact of their own actions. However, they rely on others to let them know if something is good or bad, wrong or right. If the perspectives of others clash, they are unable to resolve that conflict because there is no sense of psychological independence or having a mind of their own. Kegan gives an example of a husband who has booked a holiday with his wife. At her insistence, he booked it for just the two of them (reflecting her values), but ends up spontaneously inviting his parents when he tells them of the plan and they seem lonely (reflecting their values). In the ensuing argument with his wife, he cannot understand why she does not have sympathy for his parents. She, on the other hand, having reached the next stage and having established a set of guiding principles, cannot understand why he is so easily swayed by other people. Kegan found just over 1 in 10 adults at the other-focused stage, with another 3 out of 10 in the transition between other-focused and principled.[22]

People at the other-focused stage might hesitate to engage in upward influence without encouragement from others or consulting with others. If their espoused values are at stake, they might speak up but will worry about what other people will think of them.

TIP: If you are trying to influence someone at the other-focused stage, find out their values and frame your arguments to align with those values. To figure this out, notice what they talk about and how they frame their own arguments. Realize that it will be important to them to maintain a positive public image and have others look upon their actions approvingly.

• **Stage 4 (principled):** *Making sense of the world through your own values and principles*

Someone at the principled stage has developed an independent sense of their own values and beliefs. Instead of internalizing whole value systems, they have selected values from different systems and ideologies and crafted their own. Unlike the other-focused stage, they are viewing the world through their own lens and can judge right and wrong for themselves. Unlike the egotistical stage, that lens is more complex and includes multiple viewpoints from where they can consider the needs of others as well as their own. They are not confused if these views conflict and they do not rely on others to tell them what to do. In leadership development workshops, I often hear trainers telling participants to be authentic and true to the 'self', which assumes participants have reached the principled stage and have a fully formed 'self' to be true to. Yet according to Kegan, only around 3 out of 10 adults have actually reached this stage.[23]

The person at the principled stage is guided by a set of personal values that they have formed over the years. They will engage in upward influence based on that set of principles.

> **TIP:** If you are trying to influence someone at the principled stage, it helps to understand their principles and personal value system – something you can determine if you spend enough time with them and see the types of decisions they make and why they make them. If you have your own set of values and principles, they may respect that and be willing to have a principled debate (though some can be stubbornly focused on their own view). They would not respect you for trying to appeal to pure self-interest.

TRY THIS: Reflecting on your own stage of development

If you are trying to determine your own stage of development, think about a complex, important decision that you recently made, one that involved different people and points of view. Perhaps you were deciding whether or not to move your family to a new location, get rid of a poorly performing team

member or accept a new role that was offered to you. Reflect
on the decision process that you went through and compare
that with the descriptions below. See which one matches
your own process most closely. Remember that you are also
possibly in transition between stages.

- A person at the egotistical stage will make the decision by
  thinking only of the impact on themselves, without taking
  others into account.

- A person at the other-focused stage will want to find
  out what others think they should do. They will also be
  worried about whether people will judge their choice to
  be good or bad. They will want the final decision to be
  something that others approve of as a good choice.

- A person at the principled stage will use a set of personal
  principles or values to make the decision. They will not
  be worried about what other people think. It will be
  important to them that the final decision is consistent with
  their own values and beliefs.

Since Kegan found 6 out of 10 adults in the transition to
the principled stage or in the principled stage itself, you are

likely to be at one of those two stages of development. If you find yourself fluctuating between wanting to please others and wanting to follow your own path, you are probably in the transition phase. I spent many years in that transition and only now, in middle age, can I say that I have reached the principled stage.

Knowing which stage of development you are in can provide you with insight into how you see the world – and how your view of the world might affect your approach to upward influence.

Controlling the voice inside your head involves overcoming undermining beliefs, designing triggers to create helpful voices and finding your internal guiding voice. This self-awareness takes time and reflection, but the time invested is worthwhile. Only through working on our inner self can we create deep and sustained change that will make us more influential.

We have now explored how to be influential by managing the external and internal self – the face you show the world as well as your inner emotions and thoughts – but we do not exist in a vacuum. We exercise influence in a variety of contexts, and understanding and adapting to those contexts can be challenging.

It may be easy to learn a confident demeanour, but more difficult to adjust so that the confident demeanour does not appear arrogant in a different context. In the next section we will dive deeper into the importance of being able to adapt.

PART 3

THE SOCIAL CONTEXT

CHAPTER 5

Men Are Not From Mars and Women Are Not From Venus

As a single young woman living alone in Boston, Massachusetts in the 1980s, I often felt vulnerable. At college fraternity parties, I felt pressured into having sex; and walking down the street, I was harassed by catcalling men. So the advertisement for a Drag King Workshop caught my eye – the thought of passing myself off as a man was tempting when I felt so powerless as a woman.

To prepare for the workshop, we were instructed to dress in unisex or male clothing (I chose jeans and a t-shirt), and to make a 'penis' from a small section of stuffed tights and put it down our underwear. When we arrived, a make-up artist gave each of us realistic facial hair. I was given a goatee that, combined with my long straight hair and a baseball cap pulled over my eyes, made me look like one of the many students or part-time rock musicians living in the area. We spent the afternoon learning how to sit, stand and walk in a stereotypically masculine manner. This mostly involved learning how to spread our bodies wider than we were accustomed to and standing and walking with a slightly wider stance and a more solid gait. We even left the building and walked down the street to test out our new personas. We must have been pretty convincing because, as far as I could tell, we did not attract any strange looks.

The Drag King Workshop was a bit of fun for one afternoon and the only thing I learned at the time was the wide, solid gait. It made me feel stronger, so I adopted it when walking home alone at night. But looking back now, I realize it had a lasting impact on me. By teaching me to inhabit my body differently, even just for one afternoon, it subtly changed the non-verbal signals my body was sending. The Drag King Workshop helped me understand viscerally what I now know intellectually: that gender is a social construct, a lens through which we see the world and a performance that we can consciously manage.

This chapter explores our beliefs about gender and how these can affect our ability to be influential. There is extensive research on gender and diversity; I won't attempt to cover it all here. Instead, I will focus primarily on the aspects of gender and bias that are relevant to being influential.

How does gender affect influence?

Alice, a senior partner at a British law firm, had just moved to Hong Kong. As the new head of the Hong Kong office, she wanted to expand their local clientele and was excited to land a meeting with Mr Chan, the head of a large local firm. Alice decided to bring Brian, a young lawyer who had been researching Mr Chan's firm. Alice and Brian were welcomed by Mr Chan's secretary and ushered into his office. But when Alice reached out to shake Mr Chan's hand, he ignored her and reached out to shake Brian's hand instead, clearly assuming Brian was the boss. When Brian explained that Alice was the senior partner, Mr Chan shook her hand but did not admit to having made a mistake. During the meeting Alice and Brian noticed that Mr Chan looked only at Brian and, even when Alice spoke, Mr Chan directed his replies to Brian. Alice and Brian left the meeting feeling confused and frustrated, and Alice wondered if she still wanted Mr Chan as a client.

I suspect Alice's story will provoke very different reactions depending on your own experience. Some of you might laugh it off as something that would never happen, while others might be nodding and thinking of a time when something similar happened to them. This type of experience may not be as pervasive as it used to be, but it still occurs surprisingly often.

Such incidents are not limited to Asia, of course. Even in Western countries that champion gender equality, women often feel unwelcome in male-dominated professions such as engineering, technology and medicine. The Athena Factor[1] was a project aimed at understanding why half of women with degrees in science, engineering and technology quit their jobs in the private sector in their mid-thirties. Through surveys and focus groups, they gathered countless stories of women feeling unwelcome in their workplaces; for example, female engineers who are assumed to be administrative assistants, or technology professionals who are ignored in meetings or excluded from important insider information. One Silicon Valley executive gave herself a male alias and discovered that the emails her new male persona received were completely different from the fluff she had previously been sent.[2]

A study of 29 transgender men revealed the bias that occurs in the workplace. Those who returned to the same workplace after their transition found their male self was immediately granted greater recognition and respect. One attorney heard a colleague praising the boss for getting rid of Susan, whom he felt was incompetent, and replacing her with Thomas, the new guy whom he found 'just delightful'. He did not realize, of course, that Thomas and Susan were the same person. A professor of neurobiology at Stanford University, Ben Barres, recounted in an interview, 'shortly after I changed sex, a faculty member was heard to say, "Ben Barres gave a great seminar today, but then his work is much better than his sister's".[3]

Gender bias in the workplace can result in different outcomes for men and women. A woman might be given the most difficult clients because it is assumed she has good interpersonal skills. But handling the most difficult clients prevents her from advancing as quickly as her male colleagues. Women end up with fewer resources than their male colleagues because they are less likely to ask for more but simply make do with what they are given. Women are also sometimes evaluated differently from men, as researchers discovered in a financial services corporation.[4] Women in client-facing jobs were systematically given lower performance ratings than their male colleagues, and the women who were promoted achieved higher ratings than the men who were promoted. The raters and decision makers were not doing this consciously – they just felt the women were not good enough because they were holding them to a higher standard.[5]

It seems then, that gender has a pervasive effect on influence. Women and men are judged differently and this affects our ability to be influential both in and out of the workplace. But we do not have to accept the world as it is – change can happen, however slowly. In my lifetime, I have seen progress in gender equality and attitudes towards women. This chapter is my attempt to ensure we keep these issues at the top of our mind and continue to make progress.

Why are men often seen as more influential than women?

When one of my daughters was five years old, we were playing a computer game for which I had to choose an avatar. She said, 'choose the one in the pink dress!' and I replied, 'I don't like pink.' She looked at me with concern and said, 'but then you're not a girl!' When I explained that some girls do not like pink, I could see the effort on her face as she tried to adjust her idea of what it meant to be a girl. The incident was an example of a natural mental process in which we all engage: the desire to put things into categories.

The need to categorize things is evident all around us: in the way shops are laid out with different aisles for different products, or cities with business districts distinct from residential areas. Grouping things into categories is not only essential for creating smooth-running societies but also for survival as we try to determine whether an object is edible, an animal is dangerous, or a person is friendly. While some categories are easy to define – for example, the category 'square-shaped objects' is defined by the attribute 'has four equal sides' – humans are too diverse to be classified in this simplistic way. The categories 'men' and 'women' might seem to be defined by the sexual organs, but this does not apply to people who are intersex, transgender or non-binary.

What do we do when a category lacks a single defining attribute? How do we figure out who belongs in that category? We create a *mental prototype* of what we consider the most representative attributes of that category and use it to determine whether someone belongs in that group.[6] My daughter had created a mental prototype of 'girl' comprised of a set of attributes including 'likes pink'. When she found out I did not like pink, her logical mind concluded I did not belong to the category 'girl'.

You might be wondering what the difference is between a *prototype* and a *stereotype*. A prototype is a starting point from which adjustments can be made: 'most girls like pink.' A stereotype is an oversimplified view that assumes all members of a group are the same: 'all girls like pink.' Most people treat mental prototypes as stereotypes because they prefer clear answers rather than uncertainties. This can lead to biased perceptions, especially when it comes to influence, because of our mental prototype of leaders.

If people see you as a 'leader' or 'leader-like', you will be granted more influence. To be categorized in this way, you must be perceived as being similar to the mental prototype of a 'leader'. What is this mental prototype? Take a minute to imagine a typical leader – not a specific person, but rather a faceless, generic leader. Imagine the person's appearance, demeanour and other characteristics. If you are like most people, you probably imagined someone assertive and displaying the confident demeanour described in Chapter 2. This faceless person might also have other characteristics associated with status in society such as being part of the majority ethnicity or religion

– or being male. This is the prototypical leader, the *leader prototype* against which we compare potential leaders. While this prototype will not be the same for everyone, there is a great deal of similarity in it among members of the same culture because they have been exposed to the same history books, movies, TV and media. And, because modern societies are overwhelmingly patriarchal,[7] the male characteristics of the leader prototype are particularly deeply ingrained.

In 1973, psychologist Virginia Schein sparked a stream of research examining the male qualities of the leader prototype that was later dubbed 'Think Manager – Think Male'. She gave research participants in the US a list of attributes and asked them to assign those attributes to 'men in general', 'women in general' or 'successful middle managers'. The original 1970s studies – and subsequent studies in the 1980s – found that the attributes of a typical manager strongly correlated with the attributes of men, but not women (hence, Think Manager – Think Male). Twenty years later, in the 1990s, she found no change in the responses from American men, but American women now perceived more similarity between managers and women as well as men. This was not because their view of managers had changed – it was because they had adjusted their view of women. Schein concluded that, since attitudes among American men had not changed and men are often the decision makers in hiring and promotion decisions, the increase in women in leadership positions over the previous twenty years would not have happened without equal-opportunity legislation.[8]

What about the rest of the world? In 2001 Schein reviewed the preceding decades of research in which 'Think Manager – Think Male' was tested internationally among management students in the UK, Germany, China and Japan. [9] The management students – both male and female – exhibited a moderate-to-strong bias towards associating successful managers with male attributes (assigning similar attributes to 'men in general' and 'successful middle managers'), but not female attributes. Based on the leader attributes that appeared across all countries tested, Schein identified an *international leader prototype*, comprised of the attributes listed below, most of which (except for 'competent') the study participants associated more closely with men than women:

- *Leadership ability*
- *Ambition*
- *Competitiveness*
- *Desiring responsibility*
- *Skilled in business matters*
- *Competence*
- *Analytical ability*

The leader prototype is not only male – it includes other attributes that we associate with status in society. The lack of diversity in senior leadership is partially due to the fact that some people are biased against thinking of a disabled person, someone from an ethnic minority, a woman or even a self-effacing, softly spoken man as leadership material. If you belong to any of these groups, it does not mean you cannot be leader-like and influential – it just means you have to work harder at being recognized for your accomplishments and managing your image. For women, however, there is an additional barrier to influence, which is the gender stereotype.

> **TIP:** If you do not fit the leader prototype, do not be discouraged. The advice in this book is designed to help you. In particular, hone your non-verbal communication skills and confident demeanour (Chapters 1 and 2) and build your bases of power (Chapter 3).

Debunking the myth of the male and female brain

Before we explore the gender stereotype in more depth, it is important to first debunk the myth that men and women have innate, genetic differences in ability. This remains a widespread misconception, encouraged by the popular media, and one that I believed myself until I started looking into the academic research. Why are we so willing to believe this myth? Because gender stereotypes are so deeply ingrained in our everyday lives that we are essentially primed to believe in these differences.

Psychologist Cordelia Fine, in her book *Delusions of Gender*, uses a clever thought experiment to convey how the categories 'female' and 'male' are treated as the fundamental distinction in human society. She asks us to imagine that we can tell at birth if a baby is right-handed or left-handed. Then imagine that left-handed babies are dressed in pink and right-handed babies dressed in blue. As they grow older, they continue to wear different clothing and hair styles, with right-handed children restricted to short hair and never allowed to wear colourful accessories. Right-handers and left-handers are given different types of toys and are often distinguished verbally, with adults saying, 'come on left-handers!' or 'go and ask that right-hander if you can have a turn on the swing.' They are physically segregated on sports teams, in public toilets and even in some schools, and they often choose different careers.[10]

If you replace 'left-hander' with 'girl' and 'right-hander' with 'boy', you can see that this is how we handle gender categories – and why we grow up thinking there is something fundamentally important about this distinction. It is not surprising then that children become 'gender detectives', trying to determine, as my daughter did, what it means to be one versus the other. We do not realize how actively children are drawing these conclusions – and sometimes they do not realize it either. Several years ago we had a faulty hot water boiler that needed regular adjustments. One morning, I adjusted the boiler pressure and told my husband that I had taken care of it. My six-year-old daughter overheard us and exclaimed, 'I thought girls couldn't fix things.' When I asked, 'what made you think that?', she could not immediately explain. After a while we figured out it was because, whenever we hired people to fix things, they were always men. It was interesting to me that she did not realize how she had come to that conclusion until I asked her to think about it.

Children even become 'gender police', mocking or scolding other children for playing with toys or wearing clothes that are seen as gender inappropriate. My four-year-old daughter loved to wear Spiderman underwear and was upset when one of her male classmates insisted she was a boy because only boys wear Spiderman underwear. I assured her that girls can wear Spiderman clothes as well.

If most of us have grown up as 'gender detectives' and 'gender police', it is no wonder that we so easily believe the argument that there are innate differences between men and women, and therefore differences in their ability to be influential or work in certain types of career. Proponents of this argument claim that male brains are better at thinking systematically and female brains are better at thinking empathically, making women less suitable for careers in science and technology. Fine expertly takes apart this argument by presenting the scientific evidence and revealing its flaws. Study by study, she dissects the evidence that scientists such as Steven Pinker, Simon

Baron-Cohen and Louann Brizendine[11] use to 'prove' that women are better at caregiving and men are better at science.

I was particularly interested to read about a study that I had seen in the media, where female monkeys chose to play with dolls instead of cars. Since monkeys are not subject to the cultural influences that human children are, if female monkeys prefer dolls, there must be an innate difference. However, Fine reveals that the study was misrepresented in the media (as many of these studies are) and in fact female monkeys chose to play with a doll *and* pan[12] slightly more than with a police car and ball. When time spent with the doll was separated from time spent with the pan, it turns out there was no difference. Girls are not innately more nurturing than boys. Male monkeys, by the way, played with the doll and pan just as much as with the police car and ball. In fact, if we look to primates for evidence of innate sex differences, we see the opposite. While primate societies have clearly defined gender roles, those roles vary greatly depending on the species. In some species, males are not involved in caregiving at all, while in other species males are the primary infant caregivers. This variation suggests that gender differences are learned rather than innate.

Why do we focus so much on differences when we have more similarities, so much so that neuroscientists cannot even identify an individual brain as male or female? The cynical answer is that promoting these beliefs helps justify inequalities in the system.

If we believe that men are innately better at science or technology, we need not be concerned that there are so few women in those careers. The less cynical answer is that differences are interesting and, like the children we once were, we are still 'gender detectives' at heart. Hanging out with others of our own sex and making generalizations about gender can give us a sense of belonging, one that can transcend ethnicity and other differences. And if scientists tell us these differences are innate, it makes that bond with our own sex even stronger. But if we stop to look at the evidence around us – really look at it, not through the biased lens of gender expectations – we can see the truth for ourselves.

I used to believe that mothers are naturally better than fathers at bonding with and comforting their babies because women produce the hormone oxytocin, which is associated with developing social bonds. This was proven wrong when our second child was born. By then, I was in the third year of a five-year PhD programme and was spending all of my time at university or at my computer at home. My husband was the full-time parent taking care of our toddler and baby. I discovered that when the baby started crying, I could not calm her down – I had to give her to my husband, who always managed to settle her right away. What I thought was a biological fact turned out to be the result of a cultural practice. Culturally, mothers spend more time with their babies than fathers do and therefore they are better at calming down the babies when they cry. In my household, we had overturned that cultural practice and it was my husband who spent more time with the baby – he was therefore the one who could calm her down when she cried. It also turns out men produce oxytocin too.

While there are individual differences in our ability to empathize or systematize, there is no genetic advantage for either sex. The problem is that there is a socially constructed advantage. Many people *believe* that men are better at mathematical intelligence and women are better at emotional intelligence, that men are better at earning money and women are better at nurturing children, and those beliefs and expectations end up creating differences. Girls and boys learn from a very young age that society has different expectations of them. They learn this from parents, teachers, TV, movies, the internet, books and other children. With such clear and consistent messages from the moment they are born, it is no wonder these expectations often become reality. As we saw in Chapter 4, these expectations can affect women's performance in male-dominated fields by creating stereotype threat. If we are to reach our potential, we need to understand those stereotypes and how they are holding us back.

How gender stereotypes limit our potential

Most of us have experienced the effects of gender stereotypes in our everyday lives. If you were a girl who was told, 'stop being so bossy', or a boy who was told, 'don't cry – be a man,' you know what it feels like to have your behaviour constrained by these stereotypes. If I told you to write down these beliefs, these 'rules' for being a woman or a man, the chances are you would be able to do so fairly easily – and your list would look similar to those of other men and women.

Researchers label these gender stereotypes *agentic* and *communal*. Men are *agentic*; that is, they are the agent who is in control, they are strong, decisive and assertive. Women are *communal*; that is, they care about the group or community, they are supportive, kind and sympathetic. If these were simply stereotypes, presenting an overly simplistic view of a group of people, that would be harmful enough – but these stereotypes have become embedded as rules that restrict the behaviour of both sexes. That is, women are *supposed to be* supportive and caring and men are *supposed to be* strong and in control.[13]

These stereotypes cause problems for everyone. Men who choose to work in caregiving jobs such as nursing or social work often feel pressured to move into more administrative leadership roles, even if those roles do not interest them. In contrast, women find it difficult to rise to those same leadership roles, resulting in a dearth of women at the top of organizations – even in female-dominated industries such as primary school teaching, social work, nursing and other health care occupations.[14]

This invisible barrier preventing women from rising to the top has been dubbed the 'glass ceiling'. While there are many reasons for this barrier, including a lack of flexible work and support for women with parental duties, a factor that is not discussed enough is the one mentioned earlier: the mismatch between the leader prototype (competitive, ambitious, analytical) and the female stereotype (co-operative, caring, emotional). In 2010, management consulting firm McKinsey asked 1,500 senior executives for the reasons why women were underrepresented in the senior levels in their organizations and none of them mentioned this mismatch. The main issue they focused on was the 'double burden': that women are burdened with more responsibilities at home than men, thus making it difficult for them to work the long hours that senior roles require.[15] Yet focusing on the double burden can also contribute to the glass ceiling. A study of managers in a transport company found that women were less likely to be promoted than men because they were perceived to have more work–family conflict and therefore were a poorer fit with leadership roles.[16] In the eyes of the managers, not only did women fail to match the masculine attributes of the leader prototype, but their responsibilities at home also made them less suitable for demanding leadership roles. This is why focusing on the double burden can exacerbate bias.

TIP: If you are a woman aspiring to leadership roles, make your ambitions clear to your boss. Have a discussion about where you want to be in five years' time. If you think your boss is worried about your responsibilities at home, you could even casually mention, 'I have a lot of support at home and would be able to take on greater responsibilities.' It might seem unnecessary to be so explicit, but I have heard anecdotally about women not being considered for certain roles (that required more travel or longer hours) because the senior people assumed it would cause strain on their families.

You might have heard about a 'backlash' aimed at women who are too assertive. As with many psychological concepts that make it into popular culture, this concept has been oversimplified. In fact, backlash does not affect only women. It refers to negative judgements aimed at anyone who behaves counter to stereotypical expectations. Social psychologist Laurie Rudman found that backlash was directed at self-effacing men and self-promoting women, both of whom were behaving counter to gender stereotypes and therefore considered to be less likeable and less hireable. The problem was that while self-effacing men were considered less competent, self-promoting women were considered *more* competent (yet less likeable and hireable) than women who did not self-promote.[17] This created a double bind for women, who could not engage in behaviours that made them appear more competent (that is, self-promoting, assertive behaviours consistent with the male stereotype), without making themselves more susceptible to backlash, including from other women, as Rudman's research found.

A review of the research on backlash found that it seems to occur primarily when the woman is strong and assertive through her words; for example, bragging or verbally demanding a change. Being assertive in an implicit way – through eye contact, talking time, interruptions and an open posture – is less likely to trigger backlash.[18] Imagine a meeting where a woman keeps getting interrupted. She could respond in one of two ways: by saying, 'can everyone stop interrupting me!' or by simply interrupting back. By interrupting back, she is being assertive in an implicit way which can be perceived as being more acceptable than the first option.

> **TIP:** Practise using a confident demeanour and non-verbal signals, such as eye contact or posture, to assert yourself. For example, when students are being disruptive in my classroom, I stop talking and look expectantly in their direction. This works and does not affect my likeability. If, however, I said, 'excuse me, I'm talking here!' I would probably gain

a reputation as an unpleasant teacher. Learning to assert yourself non-verbally is useful for both men and women, but is especially important for women in order to avoid backlash.

Psychologists Olivia O'Neill and Charles O'Reilly wanted to find out if being highly agentic affected women's careers. They followed a group of MBA graduates for eight years after graduation and found that women who were both agentic and adaptable received *more* promotions during that time period than women who were not agentic or who were agentic but not adaptable.[19] Adaptability was measured as *self-monitoring*,[20] a personality trait that indicates a person's ability and willingness to change their behaviour to suit different people and situations. Women who were agentic but not adaptable may have experienced backlash (that is, been seen as less likeable and less promotable), but women who were adaptable did not. In fact, being agentic seems to be beneficial for your career, provided you know how to adjust to different situations. While O'Neill and O'Reilly were not able to look at exactly how those women adjusted, the research that I discuss in the next section suggests they were adopting a more androgynous style by balancing agentic behaviours with communal ones.

So where does this leave us regarding backlash? Backlash does happen, but not as frequently as we might think, and it can be reduced by asserting yourself through non-verbal behaviour and adapting your behaviour to different people and situations, both of which essentially soften the agentic behaviours. Sometimes I wonder if we have done ourselves a disservice by focusing too much on the backlash effect and causing women to be nervous about being agentic. The main point here is that you should not avoid being agentic – just use some of these strategies to soften or balance those agentic behaviours.

Before moving on, I want to mention the challenge that women face if they are one of only a few women in a male-dominated workplace. I have been approached by women who work in male-dominated careers (engineering or construction, for example) who told me their (male) bosses had given them feedback that they were being too aggressive or pushy. They could not figure out how to adjust and did not feel they were being overly aggressive. I watched them in the classroom and agreed, so I suspected that the judgement of their bosses was skewed by the male-dominated environment. The reason I bring this up is to remind all of us that sometimes the problem is not of our own making. Of course there is a lot that the individual can do, which is what I cover in this book. But the lack of women in leadership positions cannot be fixed by individual women alone.

One thing we can do to help change the culture that we live in is to question some of these gender assumptions. If you find yourself

– or your friends or colleagues – evaluating a man as 'too soft' or a woman as 'difficult', question those assumptions. Ask whether you or they would consider the man's behaviour 'too soft' if he were a woman? Would you or they consider the woman's behaviour 'difficult' if she were a man? Questioning these assumptions will not necessarily eliminate bias, but awareness is the first step. We can also stop thinking of certain behaviours as 'masculine' or 'feminine' and instead think of them as 'agentic' or 'communal'. By referring to behaviours in this way, we can hopefully move away from seeing them as sex-typed behaviours and make it easier for everyone to use both types of behaviour. Challenging your friends' assumptions and changing the language that you use are small changes, but if we all do them, it will have a ripple effect and together we can shift the culture to one that is more gender balanced.

Moving beyond gender stereotypes

Juliana was struggling with her new team. As an engineer, she was accustomed to being one of very few women, but this was the first time she had led a team of all men. She had tried to develop rapport with her team members but they did not seem to respect her expertise or leadership. Yesterday, she found out they had been meeting without her. When she said she should be involved in the meetings, one of them said patronizingly, 'don't worry, we can handle this,' while the others smirked. She had always thought of herself as a kind and sympathetic leader, but this team was trying her patience.

What would it look like if we combined agentic and communal into the same person? That is the definition of *androgyny*. We often think of androgyny as being gender neutral, but in psychology, androgynous people are those who are rated high on *both* masculine/agentic and feminine/communal characteristics. This rating is usually done with the Bem Sex-Role Inventory which includes characteristics considered masculine (being self-reliant, athletic, forceful, dominant, aggressive, competitive), feminine (yielding, affectionate, sympathetic, compassionate, warm, sensitive to needs of others) and neutral (helpful, conscientious, happy, reliable, unpredictable). The limited research on androgyny has found that androgynous team members are more likely to be perceived as leaders[21] and androgynous managers (of both sexes) are more likely to be perceived as transformational leaders and to have their employees identify with them.[22]

Juliana would benefit from developing an androgynous leadership style, balancing her communal qualities with agentic ones.[23] In other words, she needs to be demanding *and* caring: demanding means setting high standards and delivering tough messages, caring means providing support and sympathy. For example, when I had to manage a poor performer, I clearly laid out the standards and expectations and, with every task he did, pointed out where he did not meet those expectations. But I did this while acknowledging his efforts, providing support and caring about him as a person. There was no animosity, just a consistent message that he was not meeting the standards despite his best efforts. In the end, he concluded the job was a poor fit for him and we parted on good terms.

Juliana should think about how to be more demanding with her team and assert her control, especially since they have taken it upon themselves to meet without her. However, simply demanding that they stop meeting without her might appear petulant and cause backlash; instead, she should show the team why she is the leader, demonstrating her expertise. For example, she would have a better understanding of the organizational goals than her team and how the team's work fits into those goals. She could call a meeting where she lays out the big picture and a clear set of priorities for the team, with a timeline and specific goals.

Juliana should also balance being authoritative and participative. While she needs to show she is in control, she should also give her team the opportunity to participate in decisions that affect them. For example, the timeline and specific goals will need input from the team, since they are the ones doing the work, but she should lead the discussion and set high expectations. During the meeting, she should be aware of her non-verbal signals, ensuring she is exhibiting a confident demeanour. She could even allow the team to continue meeting without her, as long as they are able to deliver on the agreed goals.

What if you are not the leader of a team? The advice for Juliana still applies: balancing agentic and communal qualities is an effective way of being more influential. Psychologist Linda Carli and her colleagues found that women who used a friendly facial expression in combination with a confident demeanour were more influential than those who did not.[24] This suggests also that it is important for women to use soft tactics (Chapter 2), taking time to establish rapport and showing appreciation before trying to influence, for example.

Working towards solutions together

We need to work together, men and women, if we are to make progress. Unfortunately, gender issues can easily disintegrate into an us-versus-them battle. With gender differences learned from childhood, the battle lines already exist and it does not take much to ignite the first spark. Yet we are all part of the problem *and* part of the solution. Women can be just as biased as men, and men are often in positions of power where they can help women be heard and be influential.

In my Masters Leadership course at the LSE, I devote one of the ten lectures to gender and leadership. In that lecture, I share the research on gender bias, gender stereotypes and the resulting challenges for women in leadership positions. A few years ago, one of my students came to see me after the lecture. He was an engineer from Peru and told me this was the first time he had heard about gender bias. After checking with his female classmates to confirm that this was something they had encountered in the workplace, he came to my office to earnestly ask, 'what can I do to help?'

Male allies are important even if they are not in positions of power. If you think back to the anecdote about Alice, the senior partner, and Brian, the junior lawyer, there are ways in which Brian could have helped. If Brian had introduced Alice more formally, mentioning her full title, number of years at the firm and her major clients, that might have caused Mr Chan to see her in a different light. Or if Brian had kept his eyes on Alice for the whole meeting, it might have forced Mr Chan to look at Alice as well. In any case, Alice needed Brian's help and Brian needed some coaching on how to help.

In addition to working together as allies, we also need to start creating a new leader prototype by giving more visibility to female leaders – and leaders from minority groups – in the media, movies and history books. And we need to increase the proportion of female and minority leaders in our organizations by creating systems that counteract bias.

Bias is subconscious (a result of mental prototypes and gender stereotypes), so we cannot rely on individual decision makers to manage their own biases. Instead, we must adjust our hiring and promotion systems. A study of symphony orchestras in the US found that when they changed their hiring process to include 'blind auditions' (that is, behind a screen), the percentage of female musicians increased threefold from 10 per cent to 35 per cent of new hires.[25] Changing the hiring and promotion systems will have a longer-lasting effect on eliminating bias than relying on individual judgement (for more on tackling bias, see my *Forbes* article, *Why Gender Bias Still Occurs and What We Can Do About It* [26]).

We can all do our part to reduce gender bias and help make women's voices heard. A female manager working in a male-dominated organization noticed that men were the only ones speaking in her team meetings. She instituted a new meeting procedure: after a man speaks, a woman must speak before another man can speak. She told me the first few meetings were painful. The men waited in impatient silence while the women fretted about what to say. But after a while the women came to the meeting expecting to speak up and were more eager to participate and the team benefited from listening to what they had to say. This manager had to start by forcing change, but ultimately it became the new normal on her team and the women on her team became more influential as a result.

TIP: Think about how you ensure the quieter voices around you are heard. This might involve noticing who is not speaking in a meeting and asking them, 'what do you think?' Or allowing additional thoughts to be submitted by email immediately after the meeting so that introverts – who often need a quiet space in which to think deeply – can contribute. Even if you are not leading the meeting, you can still jump in. If I am participating in a meeting and I notice someone who is being cut off by others, I draw attention to it by saying, 'Emma, were you saying something?'

Gender stereotypes do not have to be the behavioural straitjackets they currently are. Being *agentic* (strong, decisive, assertive) and *communal* (supportive, kind, sympathetic) are qualities that all human beings can embrace. By embracing both, we create the space to discover our authentic self – that combination of characteristics that is unique to each one of us. And we make it possible for all voices to be heard equally.

CHAPTER 6
Seeing the World Through Cultural Lenses

When my sister lived in Taiwan, she worked for a local film production company. One day she was the Foreign Liaison and was helping her Chinese boss host a meeting with the President of HBO Asia, an American man. They took the lift to her boss's office. When the lift doors opened, instead of walking out, nobody moved – because they were each waiting for a different person to exit first. The American man was waiting, as he would in the US, for the woman to go first. My sister's boss was waiting, as is the Chinese custom, for the visitor to go first. And my sister was waiting, as she always did, for her boss to go first. I asked my sister what happened in the end and she said that her boss finally lost patience and left the lift, leaving my sister and the visitor to exit together.

This anecdote illustrates that culture is a set of unwritten rules of which we are often unaware; that is, until we encounter someone with a different set of rules. Any time you judge yourself or others by thinking 'I should…' or 'they shouldn't…', you are reflecting your cultural upbringing. Even our beliefs about how closely we should follow the rules will vary by culture.[1] Culture is the 'water' that the fish swims in. The fish is not aware of the colourless liquid around it and how it affects the way the fish swims and sees the world until the fish is moved to a different pond where the water is different. It is the pervasive nature of culture – the invisible force in which we swim every day – that makes it such a powerful force and one that you must consider if you want to be influential.

Why does culture matter? Because chances are that many of you live and work in a multicultural environment. Even if you are not exposed to people from a different country, you probably interact with people from a different region of your country, a different professional background or a different part of the organization. Organizations have their own cultures and, if the organization is large enough, it often develops sub-cultures in different departments or offices. Similarly, a school or club can develop its own culture. The culture of a group will be stronger if it has been around longer, its members do not change very often and its leaders hold clear and consistent views of the world. Professions can also develop their own unique cultures, especially those that involve additional years of specialist education and membership, for example, lawyers, doctors and academics.[2]

TIP: To determine if a group you belong to has a culture (a group of friends, neighbourhood committee

or working group, for example), ask yourself if there

is a set of written and/or unwritten rules to which

you all adhere. If there are no written rules but you all

behave similarly, that would indicate a certain degree

of culture. If there are written rules, but you do not

adhere to them, that indicates a weak culture.

Culture pervades our lives in ways that we do not realize. We interact daily with people who may have different cultural views and different expectations and interpretations. Even people in the same family can have differences that are not immediately obvious. My father and I once had a clash of views that was fundamentally cultural. A few years after I started working at the LSE, he asked me to write a reference letter for the son of one of his friends. The son was applying to the LSE, so my father felt that a reference letter from an LSE faculty member would strengthen the application. I was appalled at my father's request because, from my perspective, he was asking me to do something unethical, to write a reference letter for someone I had never met. Then I realized this was not about his personal ethics; he was simply reflecting his Chinese upbringing. Chinese culture is collectivistic, which means the needs of the group are prioritized over the needs of the individual. In a collectivistic society, your most important obligation is to your group (family, friends or work colleagues). From my father's perspective, it would have been unethical if he did not agree to help his friend's son. The fact that I did not know his friend's son seemed a minor detail to him; I should have trusted that his friend's son was worthy of a reference.[3]

The incident confirmed for me the importance of learning about cultural differences. Without understanding the role of culture, we might instead attribute these differences to personality and individual traits, unfairly passing judgement on someone and deepening the misunderstanding. Understanding culture means we can anticipate these differences and adjust to them.

The effects of culture become even less detectable when we are surrounded by cultures that are similar to each other. When we see similar patterns across many cultures, such as the fact that men tend to be more competitive than women, we might assume these differences are innate or biological, ignoring the fact that the cultures around us are all patriarchal (where men hold most of the high-level positions in society). Behavioural economist Uri Gneezy wondered if we would see the same pattern in a matriarchal society, where women hold most of the powerful positions in society. Matriarchal societies no longer exist, but he and his colleagues found a matrilineal society in India, the Khasi, where the family line descends via the mother. Even though Khasi men control the domains outside the home such as politics and the justice system, women are in control in the home. A Khasi man will join his wife's household after marriage, where he has no authority or property and is expected to work for the benefit of his wife's family.

Gneezy and his colleagues conducted a behavioural experiment with male and female participants from the matrilineal Khasi and repeated the same experiment with people from a patriarchal tribe in Africa, the Maasai, to see if men are more competitive than women in both types of culture. Contestants were asked to throw a ball into a bucket and could choose two different ways of being rewarded. They could either be rewarded a certain amount for each successful throw or they could be rewarded three times that amount for every successful throw – but only if they outperformed an unseen contestant. The second option was considered the competitive choice because it hinged on beating another contestant. The results from the patriarchal and matrilineal tribes were mirror images of each other. Among the Maasai, as we would expect in our own cultures, men were around 25 per cent more likely than women to choose the competitive option. Among the Khasi, on the other hand, *women* were around 25 per cent more likely than men to choose the competitive option. Greater competitiveness is not the result of being male: it is the result of a culture that makes one sex feel more powerful and capable than the other sex. Consistent with this, they also found that Khasi women had on average higher education and income levels than the men, whereas this pattern was reversed among the Maasai.[4]

Like the water surrounding the fish, the effects of culture on our beliefs, attitudes and behaviour is widespread yet difficult to detect. We can think of culture as a lens that colours the way we see the world and therefore the way we react to it. If we want to influence others, we must understand the lens through which they see the world. The more we can understand the lens the other person is using, the better we will be at framing our arguments in a way that allows us to be heard. To make things even more complicated, many of us wear multiple lenses from the different cultures that have influenced us: the country where we grew up, the school we attended, the industry in which we work. How can we successfully influence each other in such a complex social context? This chapter will give you some strategies for simplifying the complexity and being more influential in different contexts. I won't cover every possible context here, but I will introduce you to the concept of culture, address two cultural dimensions most likely to affect upward influence and help you boost your cultural intelligence.

How to avoid sinking like the *Titanic*

Cultural differences, like the iceberg that sank the *Titanic*, are mostly hidden under the surface. You might have put together a watertight argument, only to collide with the cultural perspective of the person you are trying to influence. Perhaps your confident demeanour appeared arrogant, like the investment banker we saw in Chapter 2, prompting the other person to dismiss your argument. Maybe you did not adhere to the culturally accepted way of presenting an argument, making it more difficult for them to follow yours. Or perhaps you inadvertently caused offence to the other person and shut down the avenues of communication. Learning to get a feel for the culture around you can help you to adjust your behaviour in order to make you more influential.

Psychologist Edgar Schein identified three layers of culture that you can picture as an iceberg, with only one component visible above the surface of the water. The visible portion is called *observable artefacts*. Below the surface are *values and norms* and even deeper lie the *underlying assumptions*.[5]

Observable Artefacts are the elements of culture that you can observe with your five senses. Imagine you have just arrived in a new city: what do you notice? You might observe the way people are dressed, how friendly (or unfriendly) they are to strangers, the layout of the streets and the types of shops and restaurants available. Or maybe you have just arrived in a new company: what do you notice? You might spot the way employees interact with each other, the way they dress, the appearance of their desks and the layout of the office. Documents such as annual reports, company newsletters and press releases can also be helpful. These observations can provide insight into the values of the company, showing you what it considers important enough to write about, talk about and display on its walls.

Rituals and language are also important observable elements of culture. Rituals are the routines that people follow, for example, celebrating employee birthdays or reserving a particular seat for the boss at staff meetings. Language includes the way people address each other, the jargon that is used or the phrases that are most commonly used. I worked in one office where we were constantly reminded of the '80/20 rule' – the idea that 80 per cent of the results come from 20 per cent of the effort – and encouraged to come up with 'back of the envelope' answers (ones that are fast and intuitive). Those frequently used phrases clearly communicated the value of efficiency and expediency.

> **TIP:** If you want to know how open the culture is to upward influence, look for observable artefacts indicating formality or hierarchy, including clothing and communication style. For example, do people call the boss by their first name? Do they joke around with the boss? How are meetings conducted? If people communicate in an informal way, with senior and junior people mixing, then the culture is likely to be more open to upward influence than one where formality is emphasized and senior people are deemed unapproachable.

Be careful of jumping to conclusions based on your observations, however. If you are not familiar with the culture, you might misinterpret it based on your own cultural perspective. When I lived in Hong Kong, Western visitors would sometimes complain to me about how rude the locals were because they rarely apologized for bumping into you. I had to explain that when you grow up in one of the most densely populated cities in the world, with whole families living in studio apartments, physical contact with other people is a normal part of life. Bumping into strangers is so unremarkable that people often do not notice when it happens. Observable artefacts can be helpful, but be sure to double-check your conclusions with someone immersed in that culture. If you join a new office and notice the boss keeps her door open, you might conclude she is open to hearing your ideas. But confirm that with a colleague first. You might find out the boss's open door is not a welcome sign but rather a necessity because of poor ventilation.

Values and Norms are the widely accepted beliefs about right and wrong. The term 'norms' comes from the sociological term 'social norms' and refers to the written and unwritten rules about how people should think and act. Should we be co-operative or competitive? Should we prioritize the needs of the individual or the group? Is it more important to follow procedures or take shortcuts to save time? These are value judgements that will vary by culture. Your attempts at upward influence will be more effective if you can frame them in a way that is consistent with the values of the culture in which you are operating.

Values and norms are hidden under the surface and cannot be easily observed. If you want to learn the values and norms of a particular country, there are plenty of books available (see the Resources section of this book on page 252). If you want to learn the values and norms of an organization, you will need to spend time in the organization, observing and speaking to long-time employees. Reading the values statement on the organization's website will not tell you much. Just because they have stated a set of values does not mean those values have actually taken hold. Culture is the sum total of the individuals in the group – it cannot be mandated by a small group of leaders.

> **TIP:** To find out the values and norms of an
> organization, talk to people who have worked there
> a long time. Here are some questions you could ask
> (you don't have to ask them all, of course):[6]

> **Q** What is the core mission and what are the goals
> of the organization? What does the organization
> do to meet those goals and how does it measure
> its success?

- Align your proposal with these goals and
core activities.

————————————

Q **What are the criteria for achieving status and
power: who gets promoted and why? Who is
respected and why? Who is not respected
and why?**

- Use this information to work out the best person to
approach (job title might not be the best indicator
of who the key decision maker is) and use the
criteria for status and power to work out how to
make your proposal more likely to be accepted. If
people are respected for their education, emphasize
yours (or get someone who went to the right
university to endorse your proposal). If people are
respected for gathering support from certain parts
of the organization, spend time securing that first.

————————————

Q **Tell me about a time when you tried to influence
the senior managers (for example, suggested a new
idea, gave them feedback). How did they react?**

- Think about what you would do if you received
this reaction. Collect the additional information
or support that you might need.

————————————

Asking similar questions to people in different roles can also be revealing. If everyone has a different view, especially on the mission and goals, it suggests that the organization is comprised of multiple sub-cultures rather than one overarching culture. The values and norms might differ by office or department, so be sure you are gathering information about the relevant part of the organization.

Underlying Assumptions are deep-seated beliefs that underlie the values and are so deeply ingrained that individuals are often not conscious of holding them. How do you uncover a belief that is not conscious? The cultural researcher, Fons Trompenaars, suggests that we choose one of the important unwritten rules of a culture and dissect it with the help of someone from that culture. He says to ask 'why?' and keep asking 'why?' until that person gets annoyed.[7] Their annoyance indicates you have reached an underlying assumption (do not do this with the person you are trying to influence! Do this with someone else from that culture in order to understand the culture).

Let me give you an example. Growing up in the US, my younger sisters did not call me by my name; instead, they followed the Chinese tradition of calling older siblings by a title. Instead of calling me 'Connson', they called me *'jie jie'* (eldest sister). You can imagine how embarrassing this was as we tried to fit in with the other children. In the 1970s, Greenwich, Connecticut was not a particularly diverse community and we were painfully aware of being different. If I had asked my mother back then for the assumption underlying this cultural practice, this is the conversation we would have had:

Me: Why did you make my sisters call me *jie jie* when none of our friends were doing that?

My mother: To show you respect.

Me: Why did my sisters have to show me respect?

My mother: Because you are older.

Me: Why did they have to show me respect for being older? I am only three years older.

My mother (annoyed): Aiyah! You don't understand anything! (This is what she always said when I asked her a question she couldn't answer.)

Her annoyance would have signaled that I had hit the underlying assumption: that even the smallest age difference deserves respect. But because she had never questioned this belief herself, she would have been unable to respond when it was questioned and because the belief is fundamental to her value system, the annoyance and dismissal would be a way of defending her value system.

> **TIP:** To uncover underlying assumptions in an organization, here are some questions to consider. After working in an industry or organization for a

while (maybe six months or more), you might be able
to answer these questions yourself: [8]

**Q What is considered the basis of truth? Does it come
from data or gut feelings?**

- If data, collect enough convincing data to support
  your argument. If gut feelings, get the views of
  respected and experienced people and use their
  'gut feelings' as proof that your proposal is good.

  _____

**Q What is the nature of time? That is, do we focus
on the short term or long term? How much planning
is needed?**

- Develop the timeline of your proposal accordingly.

  _____

**Q What are the beliefs about human motivation?
Do most of your colleagues assume workers
are motivated by the work itself or by the
external rewards?**

- If your proposal involves motivating people,
  design it to be consistent with their beliefs about
  human motivation. Or, if you want to challenge
  that assumption, acknowledge the assumption
  and collect evidence to argue against it.

  _____

These are only suggestions for the types of things to think about. To uncover other underlying assumptions, choose one of the organization's important unwritten rules and try the 'Why?' exercise.

Rethinking the underlying assumptions of your business can sometimes lead to competitive advantage. The online shoe company, Zappos, decided their core value was going to be excellent customer service. As a result, they questioned the underlying assumption of many online businesses: that the call centre is an expense to be minimized and that call operators should have their performance measured by the number of calls they complete in a day. Zappos saw the call centre as a marketing opportunity and encouraged their operators to spend as much time as needed to satisfy potential customers, even helping them find products on competitors' websites if Zappos did not have them in stock. Changing the underlying assumption that marketing is separate from customer service altered the way they approached this part of their business and paid off in the end. Even though they did not spend as much money as their competitors on traditional marketing channels, their business grew quickly thanks to word-of-mouth from satisfied customers.[9]

How can you avoid sinking like the *Titanic*? Be aware of the three layers of the cultural 'iceberg' – observable artefacts, values and norms, and underlying assumptions – and use them to understand the culture of the organization or group you are dealing with. But what about the individuals in the group? Let's examine the different types of lenses they – or you – might be wearing and how that affects your influence strategy.

What kind of lens are you wearing?

When I first became a training manager, I avoided teaching cross-cultural management. Teaching cultural differences, it seemed to me, involved teaching a bunch of stereotypes and the last thing I wanted to do was start stereotyping people from different countries. But I eventually realized that if we do not understand the dimensions on which cultures might differ, we might blame misunderstandings on people rather than cultures (such as thinking that my father was unethical rather than realizing he was viewing the world through a different cultural lens). So now I teach cultural differences, but I explain that culture is not a box. People do not fit into neat little cultural boxes. Culture is a lens and even people from the same culture might have different variations of that lens.

Cultural differences are often measured with questionnaires which generate a score (cross-cultural researcher Geert Hofstede has created an interactive website that uses data from his research for country comparisons[10]). The overall score a country is given is simply the average of the scores of people surveyed in that country. So when we say, for example, that Germany has a more individualistic culture than India, we are saying the average score of all Germans who took the individualism survey was higher than the average score of all Indians who took the same survey. We are *not* saying that all Germans are more individualistic than all Indians. There will be Germans at either end of the bell curve for their country. You do not know if the person you are dealing with is an outlier or representative of the average, so keep an open mind. What you are trying to determine is whether their lens is different from yours. If it seems as if I am repeating this message a lot (that is, don't assume everyone fits the cultural stereotype), it is because it can take a lot of repetition for it to sink in. We love simplifying the world – it takes effort to remember how complex it really is.

While there are many cultural differences that have been studied and measured (more than twenty that I am aware of), two cultural lenses are particularly relevant to upward influence: *power distance* and *communication candour*.

Power Distance: speaking truth to power in culturally appropriate ways

Victor was worried about his boss's plan for upgrading the
financial management system in the Kuala Lumpur office
of the international charity where he worked. Victor had
been through a similar experience in his previous company
and had seen how disastrous the results had been: invoices

were lost, vendors left unpaid and clients enraged by the chaos. He could see some of the same mistakes being made here. But Victor was only one of eight members of the team working on this upgrade project and his boss had never asked for his input. Even if he had been asked for his views, Victor did not want to be seen to be criticizing his boss. He kept his concerns to himself.

Cultures (and people) can vary from low Power Distance at one extreme to high Power Distance at the other extreme. Low Power Distance means that the culture (or person) has a more egalitarian attitude. This does not mean that behaviour is always egalitarian, but rather that equality is valued and prioritized. High Power Distance means the culture (or person) is more accepting of hierarchy and the authority of people in power. In those cultures, everyone knows their place and there are clear roles and responsibilities at every level of the hierarchy. Younger siblings know they can rely on older siblings to take care of them and children know they should never question the authority of their parents. Remember, however, that these cultural comparisons are relative. There is no absolute 'high' or 'low' – the important distinction is whether the Power Distance of the person you are dealing with is at the higher or lower end of the scale relative to your own. This relative difference will help you determine how to approach upward influence.

• In higher Power Distance cultures, upward influence requires caution and respect

In the introduction to this book, I mentioned a time when as a young adult, I tried to convince my parents to let me make my own decisions. If I had understood Power Distance back then, I would have approached the interaction differently. China, like much of the world, is higher in Power Distance than the US. My parents had been raised with a respect for and acceptance of hierarchy and saw the world through that lens (my mother, having grown up in the Philippines, came from an even higher Power Distance upbringing than my father, who grew up in China). Rather than using my own lens to criticize their approach to parenting and demand a change, I should have tried to see the situation from their perspective.

To start with, I could have opened the family meeting by expressing appreciation to my parents for attending the meeting. Some parents from higher Power Distance cultures might have been offended at their children calling a meeting ('I'm being bossed around by my children?!') and might have refused to attend. An important part of cultures higher in Power Distance is the granting of status or 'face' to the person who has more power. This is often done ritualistically, such as seating them at the head of the table or letting them speak first. In my case, I could have praised my parents for their intelligence and accomplishments (both had PhDs and my father was a successful businessman) and thanked them for the support they had shown us and the many ways in which they were not traditional Chinese parents, giving us more freedom and trust than other parents might have. This sincere appreciation would have also tapped into Cialdini's principle of Liking (see more on this in Chapter 2).

Then I could have shown them that I understood their role and responsibility. From their perspective, as parents they were supposed to be in control and be held responsible for their children's actions, including any mistakes. Using Cialdini's principle of Consistency, I could have asked them about their aspirations for us. Did they want us to live independently after graduating from university? Did they want us to be able to make intelligent choices in our lives? Until eventually we reached the point where I could have suggested that now was the time for us to start learning how to make those intelligent choices, while we were still under their care and guidance. Perhaps we might have agreed a process where they would have explained their decisions to us, progressing to a point where we could have jointly agreed decisions that affected us, and maybe eventually have been allowed to make our own decisions after consulting with them. It would have been a much slower path to independence than my original plan, but at least we would have been moving in the right direction. Instead, I chafed at their authoritarian attitude and concluded they were terrible parents. I resented their control and ended up doing whatever I wanted behind their backs. It took many years for our relationship to recover.

TIP: If the person you want to influence is higher in Power Distance than you are or if the culture around you is relatively high in Power Distance, then proceed with caution. Upward influence could be perceived as a threat to the natural order where the boss influences employees, not the other way around. Find ways to help that person grant your request while also maintaining their status in the eyes of others. In some cases, it might mean convincing them the idea was theirs to start with. Or enlisting the help of someone they respect to plant the idea in their head or show support for you.

Dealing with a higher Power Distance person also means showing appropriate deference and respect. A confident demeanour is important but you will need to soften it to avoid looking like you are trying to threaten or diminish their power in any way. Adjust your posture so you are not taking up as much space as the more senior person and convey confidence through your voice (Chapter 2). Use soft and rational tactics (Chapter 2) such as sincerely praising them and providing data in an objective way, and ensure that you have a relationship of trust (Chapter 3).

In higher Power Distance cultures, status is often based on age, gender (biased in favour of men) and organizational rank. If you are young, female or very junior, engaging in upward influence may be even more challenging.

TIP: Here are a few strategies you can try:

- Elevate your status by gaining the support of someone senior that the person you are trying to influence respects and getting that person to endorse your idea.
- Demonstrate your expertise in your arguments. Prepare twice as hard as anyone else and know your facts and figures.
- Build your expert and referent bases of power (Chapter 3) as much as possible before attempting upward influence. If you have the choice, bring your proposal to the person with whom you have the most expert or referent power.

• In higher Power Distance cultures, employees may be hesitant to speak up

If you are the boss who is trying to get employees to speak up, your strategy should be different. Because upward influence is not widely accepted in higher Power Distance cultures, those employees might fear retaliation. Like the Asian consultants that I mentioned in the introduction, they may expect that talking back to their bosses will be a 'career-limiting' move. Even in relatively low Power Distance cultures, employees may be reluctant to speak up. Nearly 40 per cent of American and Canadian employees across a range of industries told researchers they did not feel they should challenge their bosses and another 30 per cent said they would only offer their views if their bosses asked them (the remaining 30 per cent were willing to speak up without being asked).[11]

If you, in your role as the boss, are trying to create a more participative culture, try these strategies:

- First, be aware that being participative might be perceived as being 'weak' in some higher Power Distance cultures since the boss is expected to be decisive and in control. Show that you are in charge by using a confident demeanour and explaining that you have chosen to use a more participative style because it leads to a better outcome (not because you do not know the answer).
- Explain your expectations and rationale. If you want them to participate in decision making and argue with you when they disagree, explain what you want them to do and why it is important. A convincing rationale ('I have found this leads to a better decision') will help them understand why they should take the risk.
- In that first meeting, enlist one or two willing people to start it off. If you react positively, welcoming their input and showing

appreciation for disagreeing with you, the others will slowly start to come around. If you react defensively in any way, it will only confirm their fears and they will shut down. Depending on the amount of reluctance that you encounter, you might need to actively enlist volunteers for a few more meetings before the participative culture takes hold.

For Victor, working in an international charity in Malaysia (a country that scores higher than most other countries in Power Distance) makes it difficult for him to know if his boss will be open to upward influence. Even if his boss comes from a relatively low Power Distance culture, he might have adopted a higher Power Distance attitude from living in Malaysia. Regardless, Victor should attempt to speak up and help his company avert potential disaster. He could approach his boss by saying something like, 'I went through a similar experience upgrading the system in my previous company. There are some things I learned that might help us do things better here. Would it be helpful if I shared them with you? I could write them down or share them with you in a short meeting.' If his boss seems too complacent about the upgrade process, Victor could even add, 'we made some big mistakes in my last company and what we learned from those mistakes could help us here.' By raising it privately with the boss, he allows the boss to decide if he wants advice and if the advice will be useful. If it is not useful, the boss can ignore it. Either way, Victor will feel better for having taken some action and he will be perceived by the boss as someone who tried to help.

What about lower Power Distance cultures? The tips in this book are essentially aimed at people in lower Power Distance cultures, which is where most of the research has taken place (that is, in North America and other English-speaking countries). As I explained in the introduction, upward influence can be beneficial in lower Power Distance cultures, where it is often seen as a sign of leadership capabilities. However, even if the environment is conducive to upward influence, the other person might not be as open as you expect. Hofstede found that there can be a great deal of variation in lower Power Distance cultures, with some of the population subscribing to authoritarian values.[12] Be sure to do your research in advance, finding out the other person's attitude towards upward influence and their views on the topic you wish to raise.

> **TIP:** If the person you are trying to influence is at the lower end of the Power Distance scale, you will not need to show deference (it might come across as being sycophantic) and you do not need to get the support of someone senior (it might look like you are going over their head and using hard tactics). Instead, use the influence strategies described in Chapter 2, such as crafting a rational argument and establishing rapport.

Communication Candour: understanding the meaning behind the words and signals

Phoebe could not understand why she still had not heard from her counterpart in the Tokyo office. During the conference call, Haruto had seemed hesitant about delivering the data requested, admitting it would be difficult, but he hadn't actually said 'no'. Phoebe had tried to dig deeper, asking why it would be difficult and if she could help, but her questions were met with an awkward silence. In the end, she simply set a deadline and said, 'let me know if you have any problems meeting this deadline.' Now it was ten days past the deadline and she had not heard from Haruto. She had been emailing and calling, but he seemed to be avoiding her.

Cultures (and people) can differ in communication candour, varying from a more direct or 'Low Context' style to a more indirect or 'High Context' style. Low Context (more direct) means you do not need to know the context in order to understand the meaning (for example, 'close the window'). High Context (less direct) means you must know the context in order to understand the meaning ('it's getting cold in here'). Of course there is also a range of possibilities in between these two extremes ('would you mind checking if the window is closed?' or 'did someone leave the window open?'). This cultural difference was first observed by anthropologist Edward T. Hall who did not use a questionnaire but instead noted relative differences between cultures based on his observations.[13]

Communication candour is relevant for upward influence because it can affect your ability to understand the true reaction to your influence attempt. Dealing with cultures or people who are more direct is fairly straightforward: they will tell you what they think of your proposal, and your job is to work with that feedback (and try not to get offended if the criticism is particularly harsh). But with cultures or people who are less direct, you might not know when your proposal has been rejected. British culture is generally less direct than that in the US and some European cultures.[14] This has spawned an amusing table which you can find on the internet that explains 'What the British Say, What the British Mean, and What Others Understand' (I have checked it with English friends who assure me the table is accurate).[15] For example, you might be pleased to be told that your proposal is 'brave' or 'very interesting', when in fact you should be disappointed. Hence the misunderstandings that can arise when dealing with a less direct culture.

Why can't everyone just tell you honestly what they think? As someone raised in the US, I used to wonder this when interacting with my Chinese relatives. But then I learned that less direct cultures communicate in that way to preserve social harmony. Criticism is disguised in order to avoid confrontation and your ability to decode these messages is often an indicator of maturity. When my daughters were around five and seven years old, my mother-in-law said to them after dinner one night, 'shall I put your plates in the sink then?' The girls, who had already left the table and were watching TV, cheerfully replied, 'Okay!' Most adults laugh when I tell this story because they understand what my mother-in-law actually meant ('put your plates in the sink'). My daughters laughed as well when I told them this story recently. As teenagers, they are now mature enough to understand the meaning behind the words. This is why someone who communicates in a less direct manner finds it difficult to switch to more direct language: it can seem offensively direct, implying the other person is so immature they would not understand the message otherwise.

In more direct cultures such as the US, people might avoid criticizing your proposal in order to avoid confrontation, telling you the proposal is 'fine' and then critiquing it behind your back. This passive-aggressive behaviour is different from the disguised criticism found in less direct cultures because it is meant to deceive. Disguised criticism is not meant to deceive, but it can be so well disguised that someone not familiar with that culture might feel deceived. The Japanese, for example, often say 'it will be difficult' (*muzukashii*) instead of 'no'. If you do not understand this code, you might think the person is agreeing to your proposal and be surprised when they do not deliver. Less direct cultures also rely on non-verbal signals to indicate refusal, such as facial expressions (a tightening of the lips) or posture (looking away from the person). If you are dealing with a less direct culture, you might need someone familiar with that culture to help you decode the non-verbal signals.

> **TIP:** When dealing with a less direct culture, be sensitive to non-verbal signals. If necessary, ask a colleague who is from that culture for help in interpreting them. In an interaction with a Japanese counterpart, a Singaporean negotiator was puzzled by his counterpart's heavy sigh. He went back to his office and asked a more knowledgeable colleague, who told him the sigh was in fact a very strong 'no way!' to his proposal.

In Phoebe's case, if she were to consult with a Japanese friend or colleague, she would find out that Haruto's previous message ('it will be very difficult') was his polite way of saying no. She will need to find another way of getting the data or change her request to something that he can deliver. Since she has been chasing him for the past ten days, which would have been perceived as rude on his part, she could say, 'I'm sorry I didn't understand that the data I asked for is not available. Now that I understand, can we have a different conversation? Let's revisit our common goals and talk about other ways of achieving them.' If they are going to continue working together, she will need to invest time in building their relationship, maybe even taking a trip to the Tokyo office and establishing a relationship of trust and friendship.

> **TIP:** Relationship building is important in any culture, but it is especially important in less direct cultures. The stronger the relationship, the more likely it is that the other person will feel comfortable conveying a negative message without fear of harming the relationship, and the more likely it is that you will understand the message they are trying to convey. Revisit the five dimensions of trust (Chapter 3, see page 87) and use them to strengthen your relationship.

What is 'cultural intelligence' and how can I develop it?

Cultural intelligence is the ability to adapt to a new context, to be able to swim comfortably in a new 'pond'. The better your ability to adapt, the more likely your chances of being influential in any context. In their measure of cultural intelligence, psychologist Soon Ang and colleagues identified four dimensions that can be summarized as the Head (cognitive), Heart (motivational), Body (behavioural) and Strategy (meta-cognitive).[16] You need all four dimensions for cultural intelligence.

• The Head: *Knowing how to adapt*

Knowledge about different cultures can be obtained through books, by attending a course or interacting with people from that culture. Particularly relevant to upward influence is learning how to show deference and respect in that culture. Should you wait until the other person is seated before you sit down? Use their title or first name? While this knowledge can be useful, do not assume that everyone from that culture will be the same. Two people who grew up in the same culture will not wear the exact same lens. Their lenses will be affected by the different families, schools and organizations to which they have been exposed as well as their own personalities. Use your knowledge as a starting point and be willing to adjust when you meet someone new.

> **TIP:** Learn about the ways of showing respect in different cultures. This is especially important if you will be attempting upward influence in a higher Power Distance culture. But also notice if the other person is not as formal and hierarchical as you expected and adjust your behaviour accordingly.

• **The Heart:** *Feeling able to adapt*

If you are living in a different culture (this could include working in a new industry or moving to a different region of the country), your motivation and confidence to adapt becomes important. Being unable to adapt can affect your ability to be influential in that new context. If you have the motivation but not the confidence, start with baby steps. Finding people who have similar interests is a good way to ease into a new culture; for example, joining a running club or an art club. It might be tempting to seek out people from your own culture, but that can sometimes be more of a hindrance than a help, preventing you from learning from the unfamiliar culture. The more you can adjust to the new culture, the better your chances of getting your voice heard. If they start to see you as one of them, they will be more likely to listen to your ideas. But if they see you as an outsider who is coming in and trying to change them, you are likely to encounter resistance.

> **TIP:** When joining a new culture, take time to learn and adapt first, before proposing changes. I have worked in non-profit organizations, management consulting and academia, and in all cases it took at least three to six months (sometimes more!) to adjust to the new environment. During that time I refrained from criticizing or pushing for change because I

was still trying to understand why things ran as they did. With academia, it took me a few years to fully understand the culture and grasp what I could change and what I could not.

• The Body: *Demonstrating adaptation*

The behavioural dimension of cultural intelligence requires an awareness of your own habits and the ability to adjust to new norms of behaviour. For example, if the culture you have entered is one where people stand closer to each other when speaking than you are accustomed to, it may feel as if the other person is invading your personal space. You may find it difficult to accept your discomfort as simply a cultural perspective and to resist the temptation to step away from them. You will adjust more quickly if you can cultivate awareness and acceptance of your discomfort as a reflection of your own cultural habits and things that can therefore be changed.

> **TIP:** Practise interacting with people from the other culture. Ideally, find friends from that culture so that you can copy their behaviour until the behaviours feel more natural. Be aware, however, that behaviours are often different for men and women, so learn from people of the same sex. If you do not know anyone, watch films or videos on YouTube to learn.

• **The Strategy:** *Observing and adjusting*

Be aware of the assumptions you are bringing to each interaction and adjust those assumptions – and your behaviours – based on the other person's reactions. You can think of the meta-cognitive as the part of you that is the observer. Imagine you are having a conversation with someone and they are not reacting in the way you expected. There will be a part of you that notices this, even while the other part of you is engaged in the conversation. It might be a gut feeling or a voice in your head – something that says, 'this isn't going well' and nudges you to change course. That is the meta-cognitive, the observer who monitors you and helps you adjust. When you are dealing with the unfamiliar, having an active observer, a coach inside your head, can help prevent serious missteps.

> **TIP:** Reflect on your cross-cultural interactions, especially those that leave you feeling as if something went wrong. These reflections can be done with a friend or in a journal. The point is to give yourself feedback and think about what you could have done differently. Sometimes it is as simple as realizing you should have paused and asked a question of the other person ('What is your reaction to what I just said?') rather than marching ahead with unspoken assumptions.

Culture affects our values and beliefs; it is part of our identity. The more strongly you identify with your own culture, the more difficult it will be for you to let go of that part of your identity. Adjusting to a different way of doing things requires expanding your view of yourself, understanding that you can have different cultural identities. Most of us have at least two different identities already: who we are at work and who we are at home. Thinking of culture as just another one of those identities is a first step in becoming more culturally intelligent.

But what about authenticity and being true to ourselves? If you remember the discussion in Chapter 4 about the stages of adult development, you might remember the *principled* stage. In that stage, the 'self' is comprised of a set of principles. Imagine that set of principles as a metal core inside a rubber ball. The metal core does not change, whereas the rubber layer is malleable and able to adjust to different contexts. This is the way I think of adapting to different cultures. My behaviour is the rubber layer and can be easily adjusted. But the core stays intact. For example, one of my core principles is helping others learn and grow. If I think someone will benefit from my feedback, I will offer it, even if that person is my boss and comes from a higher Power Distance culture (and even if he happens to be someone that other people fear criticizing). In reality, I was nervous about giving the feedback, but I sincerely thought it would help him. So I thought carefully about how to deliver it and, to my relief, he appreciated receiving it.

Culture pervades our lives in ways that we are not aware, affecting our attitude and behaviours, giving us different lenses through which to interpret the same situation. The more you can be aware of the lens you are wearing and try to see the world through others' lenses, the better you will be at adapting your message and getting your voice heard.

PART 4

CREATING POSITIVE CHANGE

CHAPTER 7

The Journey Continues

You now have the tools and techniques for becoming more influential: honing your non-verbal communication, growing your inner power and understanding the social context. But do not expect an overnight transformation. These techniques can be challenging and the speed of your progress will vary, depending on the opportunities that you have to practise and get feedback. Keep working at it and you will eventually see progress. You might even want to make a recording of yourself now, so that you can compare it to how you are next year or the year after.

In this final chapter, I will share some techniques for opening the channels of communication. Of course, this whole book has been about communication, but most of it has been focused on how to craft and deliver a message. Here I will cover how to listen and connect with the other person, especially when they are unwilling or unable to hear the message you have so carefully crafted. The last part of the chapter will provide an easy reference tool outlining the steps involved in upward influence and bringing together the earlier chapters of the book.

How do I open the channels of communication?

Alex couldn't figure out what he was doing wrong. In the strategy meeting, he had been unable to convince the CEO to eliminate an old loss-making product line and invest those resources into a promising new product line. This was especially frustrating to Alex because the CEO was usually open to his ideas and this one seemed like a 'no-brainer' – a strategic move that would help the company improve its profits and image. Alex had gathered the data, crafted a rational argument and presented it using a confident and friendly demeanour. He had even spoken to his fellow managers before the meeting so that, after his presentation, they expressed support for his proposal. But nothing seemed to work in this case. The CEO would not budge.

Influencing change can be difficult at the best of times, but it can be especially frustrating when you seem to be doing everything right and still bump up against an invisible wall. Sometimes, as in Alex's case, the resistance is surprising because you have successfully influenced this person before. But people are complex and unpredictable, and seemingly unrelated things can affect their perception of your proposal. Perhaps they are distracted by problems at home or they just had their own idea quashed and are still smarting from it. Maybe your idea reminds them of an unpleasant past experience or they see your idea as encroaching on their territory. In such cases, the influence strategies you have learned up to this point will not be enough. You will need communication strategies to help you break through that invisible wall and open the channels of communication.

In Alex's case, hitting a roadblock with the CEO is a signal that he needs to find out more.

Alex could request a follow-up meeting with the CEO to better understand his perspective – or even speak to the CEO privately after the strategy meeting. By doing this, Alex can gently probe without putting the CEO on the spot in front of his colleagues and the CEO might feel more comfortable about being honest about his reservations. Only when the CEO feels heard and understood will he be open to hearing Alex's proposal. Only by understanding the CEO's view completely, can Alex present his proposal from the CEO's perspective rather than his own. With a more open channel of communication, Alex and the CEO might even reach a creative compromise or third option. Their follow-up discussion might go something like this:

Alex: I could see you didn't like my proposal.

CEO: Yes.

Alex: Could you tell me more about what you were thinking?

CEO: We can't kill the old product line – that's just ridiculous.

Alex: So you feel killing the old product line would be a mistake.

CEO: Absolutely! That product line is the heart and soul of this organization.

Alex: So you see that product line as a core element of this company?

CEO: Well, it is! When we created it, we meant it to be the flagship product and that's exactly what it's become.

[Alex nods silently and waits for the CEO to continue.]

CEO: The concept had been in the back of my mind for years – I knew there was a gap in the market, but it was only when I joined this company that I invested time into making it a reality. Everyone loved it and it really made us stand out from the crowd. When customers think about our company, that's the product they think about.

Alex: I see what you mean. When people link the name of the company with a particular product, then killing the product would be like killing part of the company. And it might anger loyal customers too.

CEO: Yes, that's exactly what I mean! I couldn't have said it better.

Alex: Okay, I see the importance of maintaining that part of the company's identity. But do you think we could refresh it a bit? Make it appeal to new, younger customers? As you know, sales of the product have been stagnant for a few years now. It would be great if we could find ways to update it while still keeping the core elements.

CEO: Hmmm, yes. I see what you're saying. We might need to refresh it if sales have been stagnating. Okay, let's look into it.

As you can see, Alex spent most of the conversation trying to understand the CEO's point of view and did not attempt to argue back. His goal was to understand that point of view so well that he could explain it back to the CEO in a way that made the CEO in turn feel completely understood. Once the CEO felt understood, he was open to hearing Alex's point of view. Once Alex completely understood the CEO's point of view, he was able to adjust his proposal to make it more appealing.

> **TIP:** When you face unexpected resistance, avoid pushing harder at that invisible wall. Instead, become curious. Find out more about the reasons for resistance. Take time to understand those reasons fully and to check your understanding with the other person. Only then can you adjust your approach accordingly.

• Psychological Ownership might cause resistance

In this case, Alex has uncovered what looks like *psychological ownership*. This is when an issue is viewed by a person as being part of their identity.[1] His CEO felt psychological ownership over the old product because it was his brainchild, which made Alex's original proposal seem like a threat – not just to the product but to the CEO himself and his identification with that product. Psychological ownership can develop through various routes, including being given control over a process or product; investing extensive time, effort and attention in it; or simply becoming intimately familiar with it over time. It can also happen in any context: a parent can feel ownership over the way they run their household, a neighbour can feel ownership over the way they set up the annual street party and a committee chair can feel ownership over a particular initiative.

Of course, when it comes to psychology it is difficult to predict other people's attitudes. For example, as a lecturer I have developed several new courses, so you would think that I would feel psychological ownership for all of them. In fact, I feel very little ownership for some of them and am happy to hand them over to other colleagues, while there are others that I do feel invested in and am reluctant to let others introduce changes to. The difference lies in how much I see the topic as part of my identity as a teacher. Opening the channels of communication, as Alex did, is the best way of finding out if psychological ownership is causing resistance.

TIP: If you encounter psychological ownership, slow down and involve the other person so that they feel as though they are helping to initiate the change. That is, instead of barrelling forward with your unilateral plan for change, pause and ask for their input. Make it a joint effort. This gives them a sense of control and can help assuage the feeling of being threatened. If possible, propose smaller, incremental changes rather than one large change, especially if that large change involves destroying their creation. They might be more open to changes that are perceived as being additive, enhancing what they have created, rather than subtractive, eliminating pieces of it.[2]

Psychological ownership is only one possible reason for resistance. There are many other possible reasons why someone might be unable to hear your carefully prepared arguments. The only way you will be able to discover that reason is by asking, listening and checking, just as Alex did. When we hit an invisible wall of resistance, our first reaction is often anger and frustration but, if you want any chance of creating an opening in that wall, the most productive reaction is curiosity. By trying to understand the other person better, you open the channels of communication and build trust. More importantly, it gives you an opportunity to explain your proposal from their point of view rather than your own.

How do I avoid creating barriers to communication?

Sometimes resistance can be created by our own words and actions; for example, failing to listen or appearing dismissive could cause a communication breakdown by triggering anger and defensiveness in the other person. How do we avoid getting in our own way?

The late Roger Fisher, the Harvard negotiation expert who wrote the classic book *Getting to Yes*, explained that breakdowns in communication often result from failing to address one or more of the *core concerns* a person may have.[3] The core concerns most relevant to upward influence are:

- **Affiliation:** The need to feel a connection with others. Address this by establishing rapport and finding commonalities rather than treating them as the enemy. In Alex's case, he could have responded to the CEO's resistance with hard tactics such as appealing to other senior leaders and getting them to help him put pressure on the CEO. Instead, he chose to try to connect with the CEO and understand his resistance.
- **Appreciation:** The need to feel like a valuable person. Address this by finding merit in what they have done rather than ignoring or criticizing their efforts. Alex was able to appreciate the value of the old product created by the CEO rather than simply dismissing it as outdated or irrelevant.

- **Status**: The need to feel respected. Address this by treating them with esteem rather than making them feel wrong, bad or stupid. By speaking to the CEO privately instead of grilling him in the meeting, Alex avoided making the CEO look bad. If he had pushed him in the meeting to explain the reasons for his resistance, the CEO might have dug in his heels in order to avoid looking weak or indecisive.

Depending on the person you want to influence, some concerns may have more priority than others. For example, when approaching an insecure boss, the main concern to focus on might be status (that is, to make him feel good about himself and feel like the idea was his), though appreciation and affiliation still matter, of course.

> **TIP:** Before an upward influence attempt, consider these core concerns and plan your approach accordingly. For example, you might want to invite that person for a coffee before the formal meeting in order to establish rapport (affiliation). During the conversation, keep the three concerns at the top of your mind so that you continue to show liking (affiliation), recognition of their contribution (appreciation), and respect for their expertise (status).

I was once blindsided in an interaction with a new colleague because I had not considered these concerns and had not adopted the right attitude. I had been teaching a course with one of my other colleagues and, when the new colleague joined, he was told to become part of our teaching team. Unfortunately, he had expected to get his own course, and we had not expected to be given a third teacher. When we met to decide how to divide up the responsibilities, he started suggesting changes to the course that we did not want to make. We tried to turn down his suggestions politely until suddenly he shouted, 'you're so defensive! Why are you so defensive?' at us both. We were shaken by the angry outburst and the meeting ended shortly afterwards. Only in retrospect did I realize that we had neglected all of the core concerns. There was no attempt at affiliation as we had not built up any rapport with him before the meeting, no sense of appreciation as we had rejected all of his ideas, and unfortunately we didn't grant him status in the group as we didn't acknowledge his expertise.

The core concerns are a useful checklist of needs that will arise in most interactions. In addition, manage the voice inside your head. Instead of seeing the other person as an adversary, walk into the interaction with the voice in your head saying 'we're in this together' and remind yourself of the goals that you both have in common. Adopting this attitude will help you open the channels of communication and increase the probability of a positive outcome.

TRY THIS: Thinking about interests, not positions

Before attempting to influence someone, try this exercise that we teach in negotiation skills classes at the LSE.[4] Rather than focusing on your position (what you want), think about your underlying interests (why you want it) and those of the other person. If you do not know their interests, then try to find out either through research or by asking them directly. Take the time to write them down in advance and use them to think about different possible outcomes that would meet your overall goal. Focusing on interests ('why do I care about this?') instead of positions ('what do I want?') makes a solution that is mutually appealing more likely.

For example, Alex's position is that he wants to eliminate the old product line and move the resources to the new product line. The CEO's position is that he wants to preserve the old product line. If they focus on those positions, eventually one person has to give in and lose. Only by focusing on interests can a win–win outcome be achieved. Alex's interest is in improving the profits and image of the company that he feels is too stuck in the past. The CEO's interest is in preserving what he sees as the core identity of the company. Discussing interests, priorities and concerns opens up the possibility of a creative win–win solution.

Don't forget about the message and timing

The research on 'issue selling' found that middle managers who were trying to sell an idea to senior management were most successful if they tailored their message and chose the right timing.[5] While this might seem obvious, it is useful to be reminded of the importance of these two elements. When we are trying to influence change, it is easy to become focused on what we want to say rather than tailoring the message and it is easy to get caught up in our own sense of urgency rather than being patient.

- **Tailor the message**: You must know your audience and adjust the message for them, including understanding their goals and framing the message accordingly, collecting evidence that they will find convincing and knowing the types of objections they will have. For example, if you are selling an idea to the Finance Director, the arguments might focus on financial benefits; if you are selling an idea to the HR Director, the arguments might focus on increases in employee engagement and commitment.

- **Pay attention to timing**: Timing is everything. If your boss is in a good mood, they are more likely to be receptive. If your proposal is consistent with the current strategy, it is more likely to be considered. Be patient and wait for the right time. The common denominator among successful influence attempts is opportune timing – and the common denominator among failed attempts is a failure to think about timing.[6]

Bringing it all together

Use this last section of the book as an easy reference tool to remind yourself of the steps involved in upward influence and to help you identify those areas where you need more work – then revisit the relevant chapter(s) for more detail.

Phase 1: *Laying the foundation*

The first phase in becoming more influential is working on yourself. This will lay the foundation for all future upward influence attempts.

A. Know yourself

A core element of knowing yourself is understanding your stage of development and where your internal voice is coming from. Are you trying to please the people around you? Or have you developed your own set of guiding principles? The chapters on gender and culture can give you insight into the lenses you might be wearing. With cultural lenses, the goal is not to change them (they are too deeply ingrained) but instead to be aware of how they might clash or interact with other people's lenses. Cultural intelligence can help you cultivate this awareness and adapt accordingly. Even if you are not living in a different culture, honing your cultural intelligence can help you adjust to the subtle cultural differences that we find among different regions of a country, different parts of an organization and even different groups of professionals.

- Find your internal voice and authority (Chapter 4)
- Notice and control the voice in your head (Chapter 4)
- Be aware of the gender and cultural lenses you are wearing (Chapters 5 & 6)
- Assess and develop your cultural intelligence (Chapter 6)

B. Strengthen your mental and emotional self

To be influential, grow your inner strength and resilience. This includes managing negative emotions, boosting positive emotions, challenging yourself and honing your ability to bounce back from failure. Building your reputation (bases of power) and Circle of Influence will also boost your resilience and self-confidence. Your reputation and Circle of Influence are not static and will be affected by changes such as new colleagues or a new role. The voice in your head might change as you take on new responsibilities or experience life-changing events such as marriage or parenthood. Cultivate a practice of mindfulness to help you notice these changes in yourself and your environment. Self-awareness is the first step to adjusting, improving and growing.

- Manage your negative emotions and practise mindfulness (Chapter 3)
- Boost positive emotions and find a sense of meaning and purpose in life (Chapter 3)
- Develop resilience by seeing failure as a learning opportunity (Chapter 3)
- Grow confidence from the inside out (Chapter 3)
- Build your expert and referent power (Chapter 3)
- Grow your Circle of Influence (Chapter 4)

C. Strengthen your physical self

In addition to inner strength, being influential requires showing outer strength and confidence. Master the four channels of communication, especially the three non-verbal channels (voice, touch and appearance). Practise using a confident demeanour and videotape yourself in order to see how you are doing. Just as important as the face you show the world is the physical strength underlying that exterior. There is a growing body of evidence showing that regular physical activity is critical for our mental and emotional health.[7] Maintaining a healthy body will help you show a strong and confident face to the world. This becomes even more important in middle age, when we begin to lose muscle mass. Choose a form of exercise that you enjoy and take care of your body as well as your mind and emotions.

- Hone your non-verbal communication skills and confident demeanour (Chapters 1 & 2)
- Keep your body strong and healthy by taking part in regular physical activity

Phase 2: *Preparing for a specific influence attempt*

Once you have identified the need for upward influence, do not simply jump in and hope for the best. As I teach in negotiation skills classes, preparation is the key to success. Take time to assess the situation and prepare.

A. Know your target's perception of you

Think about how the other person perceives you. Do they respect your abilities (expert power), enjoy working with you (referent power) and trust you? If not, then rethink your strategy. Either choose a different target or get someone else to raise the issue.

- Assess your reputation in the eyes of the target: expert power, referent power, trust (Chapter 3)

B. Tailor the approach to your target

Do as much research as you can on the other person, including on their interests, priorities and concerns. If you know colleagues who managed to get their proposals approved by that person or who managed to change their mind, find out what they did that worked. Collect the information that will be most convincing and then craft your arguments.

- Think about the other person's interests, priorities and concerns and compare them to your own in order to generate multiple possible outcomes that fit with what you are trying to achieve (Chapter 7)
- Assess the person's psychological ownership of the issue and adjust your approach if needed (Chapter 7)
- Try to determine their gender and cultural lenses then frame your message accordingly (Chapters 5 & 6)
- Tailor the message and collect data that is the most convincing for the other person (Chapter 7)
- Use Cialdini's principles to prepare your arguments (Chapter 2)
- Consider the core concerns (affiliation, appreciation, status) and find ways to address them (Chapter 7)
- Pay attention to timing (Chapter 7)

Phase 3: *The upward influence attempt*

During the conversation, try to maintain a positive attitude and use effective communication skills.

A. Adopt a positive attitude

A positive attitude includes seeing the other person as a partner rather than adversary and keeping the core concerns in mind.

- Choose a trigger that will promote a co-operative climate such as 'we're in this together' (Chapter 4)
- Keep the core concerns at the front of your mind and remember to show liking for the other person (affiliation), recognition for their contribution (appreciation) and respect for their expertise (status) (Chapter 7)

B. Practise effective communication skills

Engaging in upward influence is different from a formal debate. In fact, if you are an experienced debater, you will need to unlearn that style of one-way, combative communication. You are not trying to win points in an intellectual argument and make the other person lose – you are trying to bring someone along with you so that they *want* to do what you are suggesting. Be curious, listen carefully and show appreciation and respect.

- Establish rapport in a sincere and non-manipulative way using soft tactics (Chapter 2)
- Use rational tactics to ensure your arguments stay focused on the issue, data and common goals rather than personal attacks (Chapter 2)
- Focus on interests, not positions, and seek a win–win solution (Chapter 7)
- If you encounter resistance, step back and find out more rather than pushing harder (Chapter 7)

Phase 4: *Reflecting and regrouping*

If you want to improve your influence skills, it is important to take time afterwards to think about what went well and what you would do differently next time. This could be as simple as jotting down a few notes afterwards or taking time on a Friday to reflect back on the different meetings you have had that week. Do it while these encounters are fresh in your mind; keep your notes and revisit them. Even if you forget to revisit your notes, the simple act of writing them down will help clarify what to do differently next time. Sometimes, having a verbal debrief with a friend or colleague can bring additional clarity. If the issue is an emotional one for you, it can help to get a third perspective as you might not be objective enough to judge what went well or did not go well.

- Reflect on the interaction: what went well and what would you do differently next time?
- If the attempt failed, learn from the failure and try again – but with different strategies. Perhaps you did not speak to the right person or you did not bring the issue to the right meeting. Or you got the right person but at the wrong time (Chapter 3)
- If it becomes clear the situation will not change, change your attitude. Focus on your Circle of Influence and the actions that you can control (Chapter 4)

What I am presenting here is the ideal scenario, one where you have time to prepare and are able to obtain the information you need. It would be unrealistic to follow all of these steps every time you want to influence someone. But if you familiarize yourself with these steps, you can consciously decide which influence attempts deserve that time investment and, as the steps come more naturally, you might find yourself using them more often. If you want to influence someone and you do not have time to do the research in the preparation phase, focus primarily on keeping the channels of communication open with the techniques described in this chapter. Being curious, listening and showing appreciation and respect can help get your message heard.

'A journey of a thousand miles begins with a single step'
Laozi

Making your voice heard can be difficult, scary and time consuming. But it is also a fundamental human need and one that can create positive change. Invest the time and effort in yourself and you will be amazed at how much your Circle of Influence will grow. By reading this book, you have taken the first step on your journey. As you become more confident and influential, share your journey with others and help them find their voices as well. Make your voice heard, not only to empower yourself, but also to inspire those around you.

Endnotes

Introduction: Why Does Upward Influence Matter?

1 Morrison, E W (2011), Employee voice behavior: Integration and directions for future research. *Academy of Management Annals*, 5(1): 373–412.

2 Susan Ashford and Jane Dutton coined this term and have published extensive research on it, including Dutton, J, Ashford, S, O'Neill, R & Lawrence, K (2001), Moves that matter: Issue selling and organizational change, *Academy of Management Journal*, 44(4): 716–736; Ashford, S J, Rothbard, N P, Piderit, S K & Dutton, J E (1998), Out on a limb: The role of context and impression management in selling gender-equity issues. *Administrative Science Quarterly*, 43(1): 23–57.

3 Miceli, M P & Near, J P (1984), The relationships among beliefs, organizational position, and whistle-blowing status: A discriminant analysis. *Academy of Management Journal*, 27(4): 687–705; Miceli, M P & Near, J P (1992), *Blowing the whistle: The organizational and legal implications for companies and employees*. New York: Lexington Books.

4 Hirschman, A O (1970), *Exit, voice, and loyalty: Responses to decline in firms, organizations, and states*. Cambridge, MA: Harvard University Press; Withey, M J & Cooper, W H (1989), Predicting exit, voice, loyalty, and neglect. *Administrative Science Quarterly*, 34(4): 521–539.

5 Milanovich, D M, Driskell, J E, Stout, R J & Salas, E (1998), Status and cockpit dynamics: A review and empirical study. *Group Dynamics: Theory Research and Practice*, 2(3): 155–167.

6   Whiting, S W, Podsakoff, P M & Pierce, J R (2009), Effects of
    task performance, helping, voice and organizational loyalty on
    performance appraisal ratings. *Journal of Applied Psychology*,
    93: 125–139.

7   Kipnis, D & Schmidt, S M (1988), Upward-influence styles:
    Relationship with performance evaluations, salary, and stress.
    Administrative Science Quarterly, 33(4): 528–542; Wayne, S J,
    Liden, R C, Graf, I K & Ferris, G R (1997), The role of upward
    influence tactics in human resource decisions. *Personnel
    Psychology*, 50: 979–1006; Yukl, G & Tracey, J B (1992),
    Consequences of influence tactics used with subordinates, peers,
    and the boss. *Journal of Applied Psychology*, 77(4): 525–535.

8   Schilit, W K & Locke, E A (1982), A study of upward
    influence in organizations. *Administrative Science Quarterly*,
    27(2): 304–316.

9   Falbe, C M & Yukl, G (1992), Consequences for managers
    of using single influence tactics and combinations of tactics.
    Academy of Management Journal, 35(3): 638–652; Yukl, G &
    Tracey, J B (1992), Consequences of influence tactics used with
    subordinates, peers, and the boss. *Journal of Applied Psychology*,
    77(4): 525–535.

Chapter 1: Communication Is More Than Words

1   Mehrabian, A (1971), *Silent Messages*. Belmont, CA:
    Wadsworth Publishing Company.

2   For readers interested in the original studies on which
    Mehrabian based this equation, they are: Mehrabian, A &
    Ferris, S R (1967), Inference of attitudes from non-verbal
    communication in two channels. *Journal of Consulting
    Psychology*, 31(3): 248–252; Mehrabian, A & Wiener, M
    (1967), Decoding of inconsistent communications. *Journal
    of Personality and Social Psychology*, 6(1): 109–114.

3   Awamleh, R & Gardner, W L (1999), Perceptions of leader charisma and effectiveness: The effects of vision content, delivery, and organizational performance. *Leadership Quarterly*, 10: 345–373.

4   https://www.bbc.co.uk/news/41913640

5   Antonakis, J, Fenley, M & Liechti, S (2011), Can charisma be taught? Test of two interventions. *Academy of Management Learning and Education*, 10(3): 374–396.

6   Murphy, N A (2007), Appearing smart: The impression management of intelligence, person perception accuracy, and behavior in social interaction. *Personality and Social Psychology Bulletin*, 33(3): 325–339.

7   Neeley, T B (2013), Language matters: Status loss and achieved status distinctions in global organizations. *Organizational Science*, 24(2): 476–497.

8   Gluszek, A & Dovidio, J F (2010), The way they speak: A social psychological perspective on the stigma of non-native accents in communication. *Personality and Social Psychology Review*, 14(2): 214–237.

9   Huang, L, Frideger, M & Pearce, J L (2013), Political skill: Explaining the effects of non-native accent on managerial hiring and entrepreneurial investment decisions. *Journal of Applied Psychology*, 98(6): 1005–1017.

10 Huang, L, Frideger, M & Pearce, J L (2013), Political skill: Explaining the effects of non-native accent on managerial hiring and entrepreneurial investment decisions. *Journal of Applied Psychology*, 98(6): 1005–1017.

11 https://www.rejectiontherapy.com/100-days-of-rejection-therapy/

12 Sussman, N M & Rosenfeld, H M (1982), Influence of culture, language, and sex on conversation distance. *Journal of Personality and Social Psychology*, 42: 66–74.

13 Hall, E T (1982), *The Hidden Dimension*. New York: Anchor Books.

14 Gesteland, R R (2012), *Cross-Cultural Business Behaviour: A Guide for Global Management*, 5th edition. Copenhagen Business School Press

15 Gluszek, A & Dovidio, J F (2010), The way they speak: A social psychological perspective on the stigma of non-native accents in communication. *Personality and Social Psychology Review*, 14(2): 214–237.

16 Wansink, B (2006), *Mindless Eating: Why we eat more than we think*. London: Hay House.

17 Riggio, R E (2005), Business applications of non-verbal communication. Chapter 6 in R E Riggio & R S Feldman, (Eds.), *Applications of Non-verbal Communication*. New Jersey: Lawrence Erlbaum Associates.

18 This study used a large survey data set in which interviewers rated participants' personality, attractiveness and grooming on a 1–5 scale from below average to above average. Robins, P K, Homer, J F & French M T (2011), Beauty and the Labor Market: Accounting for additional effects of personality and grooming. *Labour*, 25(2): 228–251.

19 Deryugina, T & Shurchkov, O (2015), Now you see it, now you don't: The vanishing beauty premium. *Journal of Economic Behavior and Organization*, 116: 331–345.

20 Tannen, D (1995), The power of talk: Who gets heard and why. *Harvard Business Review*, Sept–Oct, 138–148.

21 Babcock, L & Laschever, S (2007), *Why Women Don't Ask: The High Cost of Avoiding Negotiation – and Positive Strategies for Change*. London: Piatkus.

22 Gesteland, R R (2012), *Cross-Cultural Business Behaviour: A Guide for Global Management*, 5th edition. Copenhagen Business School Press.

23 https://www.catalyst.org/2015/03/16/five-things-to-say-instead-of-sorry/

Chapter 2: How to Own Your Space

1 I am referring to the research on Status Characteristics Theory, developed by Joseph Berger and colleagues. In this research, 'status' and 'influence' are used interchangeably: having influence on the final group decision is an indicator of status. See Berger, J, Cohen, B P & Zelditch, M, Jr (1972), Status characteristics and social interaction. *American Sociological Review*, 37(3): 241–255 and Berger, J, Webster, Jr, M, Ridgeway, C & Rosenholtz, S (1986), Status Cues, Expectations, and Behaviors. In *Advances in Group Processes*, vol. 3, edited by Edward J Lawler. Greenwich, CT: JAI Press.

2 Bunderson, J S (2003), Recognizing and utilizing expertise in work groups: A status characteristics perspective. *Administrative Science Quarterly*, 48(4): 557–591.

3 Fisek, M H, Berger, J & Norman, R Z (2005), Status cues and the formation of expectations. *Social Science Research*, 34: 80–102.

4 Driskell, J E, Olmstead, B & Salas, E (1993), Task cues, dominance cues, and influence in task groups. *Journal of Applied Psychology*, 78(1): 51–60; Ridgeway, C L (1987), Non-verbal behavior, dominance, and the basis of status in task groups. *American Sociological Review*, 52(5): 683–694.

5   Hall, J A, Coats, E J & LeBeau, L S (2005), Non-verbal behavior and the vertical dimension of social relations: A meta-analysis. *Psychological Bulletin*, 131(6): 898–924.

6   The non-verbal cues identified in this section are based on the following research: Awamleh, R & Gardner, W L (1999), Perceptions of leader charisma and effectiveness: The effects of vision content, delivery, and organizational performance. *Leadership Quarterly*, 10: 345–373; Driskell, J E, Olmstead, B & Salas, E (1993), Task cues, dominance cues, and influence in task groups. *Journal of Applied Psychology*, 78: 51–60; Holladay, S J & Coombs, W T (1994), Speaking of visions and visions being spoken: An exploration of the effects of content and delivery on perceptions of leader charisma. *Management Communication Quarterly*, 8: 165–189; Locke, C C & Anderson, C (2015), The Downside of Looking Like a Leader: Power, Non-verbal Confidence, and Participative Decision-Making. *Journal of Experimental Social Psychology*, 58: 42–47; Ridgeway, C L (1987), Non-verbal behavior, dominance, and the basis of status in task groups. *American Sociological Review*, 52: 683–694.

7   Dovidio, J F & Ellyson, S L (1982), Decoding visual dominance: Attributions of power based on relative percentages of looking while speaking and looking while listening. *Social Psychology Quarterly*, 45(2): 106–113.

8   Judge, T A, LePine, J A & Rich, B L (2006), Loving yourself abundantly: relationship of the narcissistic personality to self- and other perceptions of workplace deviance, leadership, and task and contextual performance. *Journal of Applied Psychology*, 91(4): 762–776.

9   Nevicka, B, Van Vianen, A E M, De Hoogh, A H B & Voorn, B C M (2018), Narcissistic leaders: An asset or a liability? Leader visibility, follower responses, and group-level absenteeism. *Journal of Applied Psychology*, 103(7): 703–723.

10 Brown, N (2002), *Working with the Self-Absorbed: How to handle narcissistic personalities on the job*. Oakland, California: New Harbinger Publications, Inc.

11 Johnson, R E, Silverman, S B, Shyamsunder, A, Swee, H-Y, Rodopman, O B, Cho, E & Bauer, J (2010), Acting superior but actually inferior?: Correlates and consequences of workplace arrogance. *Human Performance*, 23: 403–427.

12 Locke, C C & Anderson, C (2015), The Downside of Looking Like a Leader: Power, Non-verbal Confidence, and Participative Decision-Making. *Journal of Experimental Social Psychology* 58: 42–47.

13 Kipnis, D, Schmidt, S M & Wilkinson, I (1980), Intraorganizational influence tactics: Explorations in getting one's way. *Journal of Applied Psychology*, 65(4): 440–452; Yukl, G & Falbe, C M (1990), Influence tactics and objectives in upward, downward, and lateral influence attempts. *Journal of Applied Psychology*, 75(2): 132–140.

14 Kipnis, D & Schmidt, S M (1988), Upward-influence styles: Relationship with performance evaluations, salary, and stress. *Administrative Science Quarterly*, 33(4): 528–542; Wayne, S J, Liden, R C, Graf, I K & Ferris, G R (1997), The role of upward influence tactics in human resource decisions. *Personnel Psychology*, 50: 979–1006; Yukl, G & Tracey, J B (1992), Consequences of influence tactics used with subordinates, peers, and the boss. *Journal of Applied Psychology*, 77(4): 525–535.

15 Falbe, C M & Yukl, G (1992), Consequences for managers of using single influence tactics and combinations of tactics. *Academy of Management Journal*, 35(3): 638–652.

16 Brehm, J W 1966. *A theory of psychological reactance*. New York: Academic Press; Brehm, S S & Brehm, J W 1981.

Psychological reactance: A theory of freedom and control.
New York: Academic Press.

17 Cialdini, R B (2001), Harnessing the science of persuasion. *Harvard Business Review*, 79(9): 72–79.

18 Grant, A (2013), *Give and Take: Why helping others drives our success*. London: Orion Publishing Group.

Chapter 3: How to Access Your Inner Power

1 French, J R P & Raven, B H (1959), The bases of social power. In D Cartwright (Ed.), *Studies in Social Power*, 150–167. Ann Arbor, MI: Institute for Social Research.

2 While French and Raven did not define their use of the word 'referent', they give the example of someone who is perceived as a role model. Thus we can take this to mean that referent power comes from the target seeing the influencer as someone they identify with, that is, as their referent.

3 Newport, C (2016), *So Good They Can't Ignore You: Why skills trump passion in the quest for work you love.* London: Piatkus.

4 Newport, C (2016), *So Good They Can't Ignore You: Why skills trump passion in the quest for work you love.* London: Piatkus.

5 Flynn, J, Heath, K & Holt, M D (2011), *Break Your Own Rules: How to change the patterns of thinking that block women's paths to power*, p.89. San Francisco: Jossey-Bass.

6 Dwivedi, P, Joshi, A & Misangyi, V F (2018), Gender-inclusive gatekeeping: How (mostly male) predecessors influence the success of female CEOs. *Academy of Management Journal*, 61(2): 379–404.

7   Falcao, H, Chan, S & Gouveia, R (2014), Teaching Note for *Running a Tight Ship: Save the World Foundation Budget Negotiation*. INSEAD case studies.

8   Gratz, K L & Roemer, L (2004), Multidimensional assessment of emotion regulation and dysregulation: Development, factor structure, and initial validation of the difficulties in emotion regulation scale. *Journal of Psychopathology and Behavioral Assessment*, 26(1): 41–54.

9   Chiesa, A, Serretti, A & Jakobsen, J C (2013), Mindfulness: Top-down or bottom-up emotion regulation strategy? *Clinical Psychology Review*, 33: 82–96.

10 https://www.theguardian.com/lifeandstyle/2019/dec/08/how-can-you-conquer-ordinary-everyday-sadness-think-of-it-as-a-person?

11 The therapist who gave me the kindergarten teacher metaphor was Jim Lehrman, http://JimLehrman.com

12 Chiesa, A, Serretti, A & Jakobsen, J C (2013), Mindfulness: Top-down or bottom-up emotion regulation strategy? *Clinical Psychology Review*, 33: 82–96.

13 Dweck, C S (2017), *Mindset: Changing the way you think to fulfil your potential*. London: Robinson.

14 Duckworth, A (2017), *Grit: Why passion and resilience are the secrets to success*. London: Vermilion.

15 Ericsson, A & Pool, R (2016), *Peak: How all of us can achieve extraordinary things*. London: Vintage.

16 Ericsson, A & Pool, R (2016), *Peak: How all of us can achieve extraordinary things*, p.19. London: Vintage.

17 Keltner, D, Gruenfeld, D H & Anderson, C (2003), Power, approach, and inhibition. *Psychological Review*, 110(2):

265–284; Guinote, A (2017), How power affects people: Activating, wanting, and goal seeking. *Annual Review of Psychology*, 68: 353–381.

18 Galinsky, A, Gruenfeld, D H & Magee, J C (2003), From power to action. *Journal of Personality and Social Psychology*, 85(3): 453–466.

19 Lammers, J, Dubois, D, Rucker, D D & Galinsky, A D (2013), Power gets the job: Priming power improves interview outcomes. *Journal of Experimental Social Psychology*, 49(4): 776–779.

20 https://www.ted.com/talks/amy_cuddy_your_body_ language_shapes_who_you_are

21 Carney, D R, Cuddy, A J C & Yap, A J (2010), Power posing: Brief nonverbal displays affect neuroendocrine levels and risk tolerance. *Psychological Science*, 21(10): 1363–1368.

22 Ranehill, E, Dreber, A, Johannesson, M, Leiberg, S, Sul, S & Weber, R A (2015), Assessing the robustness of power posing: No effect on hormones and risk tolerance in a large sample of men and women. *Psychological Science*, 26(5): 653–656.

23 Cuddy, A J C, Wilmuth, C A, Yap, A J & Carney, D R (2015), Preparatory power posing affects nonverbal presence and job interview performance. *Journal of Applied Psychology*, 100(4): 1286–1295.

24 McMahan, E A & Estes, D (2011), Hedonic versus eudaimonic conceptions of well-being: Evidence of differential associations with self-reported well-being. *Social Indicators Research*, 103(1): 93–108.

25 Ryff, C D (2017), Eudaimonic well-being, inequality, and health: Recent findings and future directions. *International Review of Economics*, 64: 159–178.

26 Grant, A M (2008), The significance of task significance: Job performance effects, relational mechanisms and boundary conditions. *Journal of Applied Psychology*, 93: 108–124.

27 Cameron, J (1993), *The Artist's Way: A Course in Discovering and Recovering Your Creative Self*. London: Pan Books.

Chapter 4: Control the Voice Inside Your Head

1 Brauer, K & Wolf, A (2016), Validation of the German-language Clance Impostor Phenomenon Scale. *Personality and Individual Differences*, 102: 153–158.

2 Clance, P R & Imes, S (1978), The impostor phenomenon in high achieving women: Dynamics and therapeutic intervention. *Psychotherapy: Theory, Research and Practice*: 241–247.

3 Badawy, R L, Gazdag, B A, Bentley, J R & Brouer, R L (2018), Are all impostors created equal? Exploring gender differences in the impostor phenonmenon-performance link. *Personality and Individual Differences*, 131: 156–163.

4 Pauline Clance's website: https://paulineroseclance.com/ impostor_phenomenon.html

5 Badawy, R L, Gazdag, B A, Bentley, J R & Brouer, R L (2018), Are all impostors created equal? Exploring gender differences in the impostor phenonmenon-performance link. *Personality and Individual Differences*, 131: 156–163.

6 Clance, P R & Imes, S (1978), The impostor phenomenon in high achieving women: Dynamics and therapeutic intervention. *Psychotherapy: Theory, Research and Practice*: 241–247.

7 Steele, C M & Aronson, J (1995), Stereotype threat and the intellectual test performance of African Americans. *Journal of Personality and Social Psychology*, 69: 797–811.

8   Kray, L J, Thompson, L & Galinsky, A (2001), Battle of the
    Sexes: Gender stereotype confirmation and reactance in
    negotiations. *Journal of Personality and Social Psychology*,
    80(6): 942–958.

9   Spencer, S J, Logel, C & Davies, P G (2016), Stereotype Threat.
    Annual Review of Psychology, 67: 415–417.

10 Spencer, S J, Logel, C & Davies, P G (2016), Stereotype Threat.
    Annual Review of Psychology, 67: 415–417.

11 Guyll, M, Madon, S, Prieto, L & Scherr, K C (2010),
    The potential roles of self-fulfilling prophecies, stigma
    consciousness, and stereotype threat in linking Latino/a
    ethnicity and educational outcomes. *Journal of Social Issues*,
    66(1): 113–130.

12 Pinel, E C, Warner, L R & Chua, P (2005), Getting there is
    only half the battle: Stigma consciousness and maintaining
    diversity in higher education. *Journal of Social Issues*, 61(3):
    481–506.

13 Shih, M, Pittinsky, T L, Ambady, N (1999), Stereotype
    susceptibility: identity salience and shifts in quantitative
    performance. *Psychological Science*, 10(1): 80–83.

14 Rotter, J B (1966), Generalized expectancies for internal versus
    external control of reinforcement. *Psychological Monograph:
    General and Applied*, 80(1): 1–28.

15 Covey, S R (1989), *The 7 Habits of Highly Effective People*.
    London: Simon & Schuster UK Ltd.

16 https://www.goodreads.com/quotes/1227701-if-you-don-t-
    like-something-change-it-if-you-can-t

17 Martin, G (2019), *Be the Change: A toolkit for the activist in
    you*. London: Sphere.

18 My friend who created the 'trigger' exercise is Glynne Steele, Founder and Director, dothinkdo; https://www.dothinkdo.com/

19 Berger, J G (2012), *Changing on the Job: Developing Leaders for a Complex World*. Stanford, CA: Stanford Business Books.

20 Kegan, R (1994), *In Over Our Heads: The mental demands of modern life*. Cambridge, MA: Harvard University Press.

21 Kegan, R (1994), *In Over Our Heads: The mental demands of modern life*. Cambridge, MA: Harvard University Press.

22 Kegan, R (1994), *In Over Our Heads: The mental demands of modern life*. Cambridge, MA: Harvard University Press.

23 Kegan, R (1994), *In Over Our Heads: The mental demands of modern life*. Cambridge, MA: Harvard University Press.

Chapter 5: Men Are Not From Mars and Women Are Not From Venus

1   Hewlett, S A, Luce, C B, Servon, L J & Sherbin, L (2008), *The Athena Factor: Reversing the brain drain in science, engineering, and technology*. The Center for Work-Life Policy.

2   Fine, C (2010), *Delusions of Gender: The Real Science Behind Sex Differences*, p.69. London: Icon Books.

3   Fine, C (2010), *Delusions of Gender: The Real Science Behind Sex Differences*, p.54. London: Icon Books.

4   The researchers didn't reveal the name of the company; academics are required to protect the identity of their research subjects.

5   Lyness, K S & Heilman, M E (2006), When Fit Is Fundamental: Performance Evaluations and Promotions of Upper-Level Female and Male Managers. *Journal of Applied Psychology*, 91(4): 777–785.

6 Rosch, E (1978), Principles of categorization. In *Cognition and Categorization*, E Rosch & B B Lloyd (Eds.). New Jersey: Erlbaum, 27–48.

7 While there are still some matrilineal societies (where descent is traced through the mother and children take the mother's name), truly matriarchal societies (where women hold most of the powerful positions in politics and society) no longer exist. See page 1639 in Gneezy, U, Leonard, K L & List, J A (2009), Gender differences in competition: Evidence from a matrilineal and a patriarchal society. *Econometrica*, 77(5): 1637–1664.

8 Schein, V E (2001), A global look at psychological barriers to women's progress in management. *Journal of Social Issues*, 57(4): 675–688.

9 Schein, V E (2001), A global look at psychological barriers to women's progress in management. *Journal of Social Issues*, 57(4): 675–688.

10 Fine, C (2010), *Delusions of Gender: The Real Science Behind Sex Differences*. London: Icon Books.

11 In her chapter entitled 'Brain Scams', Fine tears apart best-selling books that support the neurosexist argument. She focuses heavily on Louann Brizendine's book *The Female Brain* (2008) and reveals the many errors, misrepresentations, and outright lies contained in that book.

12 It seems odd that researchers would categorize a pan as a 'girlish' toy for monkeys when monkeys (of both sexes) do not normally cook with pans.

13 Heilman, M E (2001), Description and prescription: How gender stereotypes prevent women's ascent up the organizational ladder. *Journal of Social Issues,* 57(4): 657–674.

14 Dill, J S, Price-Glynn, K & Rakovski, C (2016), Does the 'glass escalator' compensate for the devaluation of care work occupations?: The careers of men in low- and middle-skill health care jobs. *Gender & Society*, 30(2): 334–360.

15 McKinsey (2010), *Women at the Top of Corporations: Making It Happen.*

16 Hoobler, J M, Wayne, S J & Lemmon, G (2009), Bosses' perceptions of family-work conflict and women's promotability: Glass ceiling effects. *Academy of Management Journal*, 52(5): 939–957.

17 Rudman, L A (1998), Self-promotion as a risk factor for women: The costs and benefits of counterstereotypical impression management. *Journal of Personality and Social Psychology*, 74(3): 629–645.

18 Williams, M J & Tiedens, L Z (2015), The subtle suspension of backlash: A meta-analysis of penalties for women's implicit and explicit dominance behavior. *Psychological Bulletin*, 142(2): 165–197.

19 O'Neill, O A & O'Reilly, C A (2011), Reducing the backlash effect: Self-monitoring and women's promotions, *Journal of Occupational and Organizational Psychology*, 84: 825–832.

20 Snyder, M (1974), Self-monitoring of expressive behavior. *Journal of Personality and Social Psychology*, 30(4): 526–537.

21 Gershenoff, A B & Foti, R J (2003), Leader emergence and gender roles in all-female groups. *Small Group Research*, 34(2): 170–196.

22 Kark, R, Waismel-Manor, R & Shamir, B (2012), Does valuing androgyny and femininity lead to a female advantage? The relationship between gender-role, Transformational Leadership, and identification. *Leadership Quarterly*, 23: 620–640.

23 Zheng, W, Surgevil, O & Kark, R (2018), Dancing on the razor's edge: How top-level women leaders manage the paradoxical tensions between agency and communion. *Sex Roles*, 79: 633–650.

24 Carli, L L, LaFleur, S J & Loeber, C C (1995), Nonverbal behavior, gender, and influence. *Journal of Personality and Social Psychology*, 68: 1030–1041.

25 Goldin, C & Rouse, C (2000), Orchestrating impartiality: the impact of 'blind' auditions on female musicians. *The American Economic Review*, 90(4): 715–741.

26 https://www.forbes.com/sites/londonschoolofeconomics/ 2019/07/05/why-gender-bias-still-occurs-and-what-we-can-do-about-it/#4ecb2a275228

Chapter 6: Seeing the World Through Cultural Lenses

1 Gelfand, M J, Raver, J L, Nishii, L, Leslie, L M, Lun, J, Lim, B C, Duan, L, Almaliach, A, Ang, S, Arnadottir, J, Aycan, Z, et al. (2011), Differences between tight and loose cultures: A 33-nation study. *Science*, 332(6033): 1100–1104.

2 Schein, E H (2017), *Organizational Culture and Leadership*, 5th edition. New Jersey: John Wiley & Sons Inc.

3 Someone later pointed out to me that my father probably did not understand what an academic reference letter entailed, since they were not commonly used by his generation in China. He probably thought it meant a character reference, in which case I should have trusted his judgement that his friend's son was of a good character.

4 Gneezy, U, Leonard, K L & List, J A (2009), Gender differences in competition: Evidence from a matrilineal and a patriarchal society. *Econometrica*, 77(5): 1637–1664.

5   Schein, E H (2017), *Organizational Culture and Leadership*,
    5th edition. New Jersey: John Wiley & Sons Inc.

6   These questions are based on Schein, E H (1990),
    Organizational culture. *American Psychologist*, 45(2): 109–119.

7   Trompenaars, F & Hampden-Turner, C (2011), *Riding the
    waves of culture: Understanding cultural diversity in business.*
    2nd edition. London: Nicholas Brealey Publishing.

8   Detert, J R, Scroeder, R G & Mauriel, J J (2000), A framework
    for linking culture and improvement initiatives in organizations.
    Academy of Management Review, 25(4): 850–863.

9   Hsieh, T (2010), *Delivering Happiness: A Path to Profits,
    Passion, and Purpose*. New York: Grand Central Publishing.

10 https://www.hofstede-insights.com/product/compare-countries/

11 Carsten, M K, Uhl-Bien, M, West, B J, Patera, J L & McGregor,
    R (2010), Exploring social constructions of followership:
    A qualitative study. *Leadership Quarterly*, 21: 543–562.

12 Hofstede, G (1997), *Cultures and Organizations: Software
    of the Mind*. New York: McGraw-Hill.

13 Hall, E T (1989), *Beyond Culture*. New York: Anchor Books.

14 Gesteland, R R (2012), *Cross-Cultural Business Behaviour:
    A Guide for Global Management*, 5th edition. Copenhagen
    Business School Press.

15 http://www.bbcamerica.com/anglophenia/2012/01/what-
    the-british-say-and-what-they-really-mean

16 Ang, S, Van Dyne, L, Koh, C, Ng, K Y, Templer, K J, Tay,
    C & Chandrasekar, N A (2007), Cultural intelligence:
    Its measurement and effects on cultural judgment and
    decision making, cultural adaptation and task performance.
    Management and Organization Review, (3)3: 335–371.

Chapter 7: The Journey Continues

1   Pierce, J L, Kostova, T & Dirks, K T (2001), Toward a Theory of Psychological Ownership in Organizations. *Academy of Management Review*, 26(2): 298–310.

2   Dirks, K T, Cummings, L L & Pierce, J L (1996), Psychological ownership in organizations: Conditions under which individuals promote and resist change. In R W Woodman & W A Pasmore (Eds.), *Research in Organizational Change and Development*, 9: 1–23. Greenwich, CT: JAI Press.

3   Fisher, R & Shapiro, D (2007), *Building Agreement: Using emotions as you negotiate*. London: Random House.

4   http://www.lse.ac.uk/study-at-lse/Online-learning/Courses/Programme-on-Negotiation

5   I am drawing on the following sources: Ashford, S J & Detert, J (2015), Get the boss to buy in. *Harvard Business Review*, Jan–Feb, 72–79; Dutton, J, Ashford, S, O'Neill, R & Lawrence, K (2001), Moves that matter: Issue selling and organizational change, *Academy of Management Journal*, 44(4): 716–736; Ashford, S J, Rothbard, N P, Piderit, S K & Dutton, J E (1998), Out on a limb: The role of context and impression management in selling gender-equity issues. *Administrative Science Quarterly*, 43(1): 23–57; Dutton, J E & Ashford, S J (1993), Selling Issues to Top Management. *Academy of Management Review*, 18(3): 397–428.

6   Dutton, J, Ashford, S, O'Neill, R & Lawrence, K (2001), Moves that matter: Issue selling and organizational change, *Academy of Management Journal*, 44(4): 716–736.

7   https://www.nia.nih.gov/health/cognitive-health-and-older-adults

Resources

Online Resources

For more from Connson Chou Locke, go to ConnsonLocke.com

Tips on how to make the most of video calls: https://connsonlocke.com/making-your-voice-heard-while-working-from-home/

Interactive website with country comparisons using Hofstede's cultural dimensions: https://www.hofstede-insights.com/product/compare-countries/

LSE Online Negotiation course featuring Connson Chou Locke and Tara Reich: http://www.lse.ac.uk/study-at-lse/Online-learning/Courses/Programme-on-Negotiation

Overview of women's legal rights and constraints in countries around the world: *Women, Business and the Law*, available at https://wbl.worldbank.org/

Recommended Books

This is a short list of books that I recommend. I have given a brief description for each book so you can choose the ones most useful to you.

Break Your Own Rules: How to change the patterns of thinking that block women's paths to power, Jill Flynn, Kathryn Heath and Mary Davis Holt (New Jersey: John Wiley & Sons, 2011)
Tips from executive coaches on how women can assert themselves.

Cross-Cultural Business Behavior: A guide for global management, Richard Gesteland (Copenhagen: Copenhagen Business School Press, 2012)
Overview of cultural differences with a summary of negotiation styles from forty countries.

How to Have a Good Day: The essential toolkit for a productive day at work and beyond, Caroline Webb (London: Macmillan, 2016)
Tips on how to be more effective at work (for example, productivity, relationships, resilience) using research from behavioural science.

Made to Stick: Why some ideas take hold and others come unstuck, Chip Heath and Dan Heath (London: Arrow, 2008)
Six principles for how to craft a memorable and convincing story or speech.

The 7 Habits of Highly Effective People, Stephen Covey (London: Simon & Schuster, 1999)
Important insights for anyone undertaking personal change.

What Works: Gender equality by design, Iris Bohnet (Cambridge, MA: Harvard University Press, 2016)
Advice from a behavioural economist on how organizational systems can be changed to promote gender equality.

Bibliography

Babcock, L & Laschever, S (2008), *Why Women Don't Ask: The high cost of avoiding negotiation, and Positive Strategies for Change*. London: Piatkus.

Berger, J G (2011), *Changing on the Job: Developing leaders for a complex world*. Stanford, CA: Stanford Business Books.

Brown, N (2003), *Working with the Self-Absorbed: How to handle narcissistic personalities on the job*. Oakland, CA: New Harbinger Publications, Inc.

Cameron, J (1993), *The Artist's Way: A course in discovering and recovering your creative self*. London: Pan Books.

Covey, S R (1999), *The 7 Habits of Highly Effective People*. London: Simon & Schuster.

Duckworth, A (2017), *Grit: Why passion and resilience are the secrets to success*. London: Vermilion.

Dweck, C S (2017), *Mindset: Changing the way you think to fulfil your potential*. London: Robinson.

Ericsson, A & Pool, R (2017), *Peak: How all of us can achieve extraordinary things*. London: Vintage.

Fine, C (2010), *Delusions of Gender: The real science behind sex differences*. London: Icon Books.

Fisher, R & Shapiro, D (2007), *Building Agreement: Using emotions as you negotiate*. London: Random House.

Flynn, J, Heath, K & Holt, M D (2011), *Break Your Own Rules: How to change the patterns of thinking that block women's paths to power*. New Jersey: John Wiley & Sons.

Gesteland, R R (2012), *Cross-Cultural Business Behaviour: A guide for global management*, 5th edition. Copenhagen: Copenhagen Business School Press.

Grant, A (2013), *Give and Take: Why helping others drives our success*. London: Orion Publishing Group.

Hall, E T (1988), *The Hidden Dimension*. New York: Bantam Doubleday Dell Publishing Group.

Hall, E T (1997), *Beyond Culture*. New York: Anchor Books.

Hewlett, S A, Luce, C B, Servon, L J & Sherbin, L (2008), *The Athena Factor: Reversing the brain drain in science, engineering, and technology*. The Center for Work-Life Policy.

Hofstede, G (2010), *Cultures and Organizations: Software of the mind*. New York: McGraw-Hill.

Hsieh, T (2010), *Delivering Happiness: A path to profits, passion, and purpose*. New York: Grand Central Publishing.

Kegan, R (1994), *In Over Our Heads: The mental demands of modern life*. Cambridge, MA: Harvard University Press.

Martin, G (2019), *Be the Change: A toolkit for the activist in you*. London: Sphere.

Mehrabian, A (1972), *Silent Messages*. Belmont, CA: Wadsworth Publishing Company.

Newport, C (2016), *So Good They Can't Ignore You: Why skills trump passion in the quest for work you love*. London: Piatkus.

Schein, E H (2016), *Organizational Culture and Leadership*, 5th edition. New Jersey: John Wiley & Sons Inc.

Trompenaars, F & Hampden-Turner, C (2012), *Riding the waves of culture: Understanding cultural diversity in business*. 3rd edition. London: Nicholas Brealey Publishing.

Wansink, B (2006), *Mindless Eating: Why we eat more than we think*. London: Bantam Books.

Acknowledgements

This book would not exist without Claudia Connal, Publishing Director at Endeavour, who emailed me out of the blue in November 2018. As an academic, I occasionally receive emails from publishers asking if I'm interested in writing a textbook or monograph of my research. Claudia had a different vision: a book for a general readership that provided practical tools grounded in scientific evidence. Not only did this appeal to me, but her timing was also perfect. I had been thinking about writing a book and her email was the nudge that I needed.

As this is my first book, I very much appreciated Claudia's excellent editing skills. She has a knack for knowing when something needs more (or less) explanation, when a section needs more practical tips and when I lapse into overly academic language. As the manuscript grew in size, it became overwhelming for me, but Claudia managed to pick out the key paragraphs or sections that needed work.

I am also grateful to Kirsty McCusker-Delicado, Head of Masterclasses at *Guardian* Masterclasses, for giving me a platform to reach beyond the LSE community. The popularity of my *Guardian* Masterclass made me realize these concepts do appeal to the general public and gave me the confidence to develop them into a book.

My family have been my biggest supporters, including my husband and his family, my daughters, and my parents, Joseph and Lily Chou. My parents were not able to see the book published before they passed away in 2019 and 2020, but they knew that I was writing it and I was able to share with them the excitement of landing my first book contract.

Without my husband, Jason Locke, this journey would never have begun. The stable foundation of our partnership gave me the courage to set ambitious goals and his patience and unconditional support allowed me to pursue these goals. Not only did he quit his job in Hong Kong and move to Berkeley with me so that I could pursue a PhD, but he also became a full-time parent so that I could pursue a career in academia. He was the one who noticed LSE was hiring and persuaded me to apply. And he was the one who supported me in writing this book – and ensured that I had quiet time every weekend to do so.

Finally, a big thank you to all of my wonderful students at the LSE, past and present, and to the participants at my sessions at the United Nations System Staff College. I have learned so much from all of you. Your stories and experiences from around the world have given me new insights and your questions have helped clarify my thinking and improve my teaching. I hope this book helps you to get your voices heard.

Index

Author Biography

Connson Chou Locke is Professorial Lecturer in Management at the London School of Economics and Political Science where she teaches leadership, organizational behaviour and negotiation. She holds a PhD and MSc in Business Administration, with a speciality in organizational behaviour, from the University of California at Berkeley, and a BA in Sociology from Harvard University. Her highly popular *Guardian* Masterclass 'Developing your presence, power and influence' regularly sells out. Her clients include Harvard Medical School, Orange Group, KPMG and the United Nations System Staff College.

Discover more at connsonlocke.com